# The Early Literacy Handbook

Making sense of language and literacy with children
birth to seven – a practical guide to the context approach

**by Dominic Wyse and Christine Parker**

BIRTH
TO
SEVEN

## Contents

Published by Practical Pre-School Books, A Division of MA Education Ltd,
St Jude's Church, Dulwich Road, Herne Hill, London, SE24 0PB.

Tel: 020 7738 5454

www.practicalpreschoolbooks.com

© MA Education Ltd 2012

All images © MA Education Ltd., other than the images listed below. All photos other than the below taken by Lucie Carlier.
Front cover images: Left: © MA Education, top right: © iStockphoto.com/Liza McCorkle, bottom right: © (Mike Booth)/Alamy.
Page 39 © MA Education Ltd photo taken by Ben Suri

ISBN 978-1-907241-26-0

# Introduction

**Experimenting with chalk to communicate meaning**

The heart of this book is a new approach to the teaching of language and literacy: its focus is exemplary classroom practice built on rigorous theory and evidence. The writing of the book was made possible by the authors' combined experience of more than 40 years in education. Christine brings to the book most of all her wealth of experience as a nursery educator, head of early years centre, primary teacher and primary head teacher. Dominic brings his experience as a teacher, as a teacher trainer, as a researcher and, for this book, a new theory on the teaching of English, language and literacy (TELL theory[1]). But even more

than these features, we hope we communicate our undimmed excitement and passion for teaching and learning.

There are many very good publications[2] about language and literacy written for early years and primary educators[3]. But the unique contribution of our book is its particular focus on language and literacy pedagogy and the explicit ways it links with research and theory. One important strand of our approach is contextualised teaching. For example this is shown in our explanation of how teaching of letters and

---

1   TELL theory was first presented in 2011 at a keynote symposium at the American Literacy Research Association. The theory has been published in the 10,000 word introduction to the four volume set *Literacy Teaching and Education: SAGE library of educational thought and practice* (Wyse D, ed, 2011. Sage, London, UK). The theory also builds on *Teaching English, Language and Literacy* (Wyse D, Jones R, 2007. Routledge, London, UK); and *The Routledge International Handbook of English, Language and Literacy Teaching* (Wyse D, Andrews R, Hoffman J, eds, 2010. Routledge, London, UK).

2   For example: Bruce T, Spratt J (2011) *Essentials of Literacy from 0-7.* Second Edition. Sage, London, UK; and Whitehead M (2004) *Language and Literacy in the Early Years.* Third Edition. Sage, London, UK.

3   We use the term 'educator' throughout the book to describe all teachers, professionals and practitioners working to help children's learning.

# INTRODUCTION

phonemes[4] can contribute to children's reading development. Contextualised teaching begins with whole texts that engage children's interest and motivation. The most important features of texts, such as the way narrative connects with children's sense of wonder and with their everyday lives, are emphasised first and foremost. Work on the sentences, words, letters and phonemes then follows naturally because these linguistic building blocks are made naturally meaningful when children experience them in the context of whole texts. Teaching about letters and phonemes is an important component in learning to read, but there are serious risks if it is magnified above all others, especially as the focus of high stakes national testing. This is one reason why educators and parents must fight for a balanced and research-informed approach to literacy teaching.

We wanted the links between theory and practice to be crystal clear. For that reason each chapter begins with a short account of the most relevant theory and research. This is then exemplified and enriched by dynamic guidance and insights into the practice of teaching. Many of the examples were created as Christine drew on the practice of teachers in her school at the time of writing. Although practice sections come after theory sections in the book, during the process of writing we were constantly questioning and revising both to ensure that there was a genuine fit between the two.

The book is divided into three sections on: language and literacy, reading, and writing. Language is at the heart of literacy; in fact as we argue in our chapter on multilingualism, languages are at the heart of literacy in every classroom in the land. But where some otherwise admirable accounts of literacy teaching fail is in their lack of attention to reading and writing processes as important in their own right. Yes, they are connected in literacy, but effective teaching and learning requires an understanding of their distinctness as well as the links between them.

Perhaps the most important chapter in the book is "High quality literacy teaching". It is here that we nail our colours to the mast in our description of what we consider to be exemplary practice. But such practice is also underpinned by the thinking demonstrated in all the other chapters in the book. Appropriate knowledge and skills are needed by educators for each of the different phases and elements of any lesson. The sessions shown in the high quality literacy teaching chapter are not meant to suggest a rigid, fixed format (no return to the literacy hour is implied here!) Variation is a necessary part of good teaching, not least to sustain children's interest. Once again the other chapters of the book reveal the nuances that are necessary, but more important is the need for you to avoid the idea of 'recipes' and to release your own creativity and imagination for developing the curriculum. By combining messages from different chapters we hope your ideas will transcend the linear nature of this conventional printed text, just like the ebb and flow of teaching and learning that emerges from real engagement with children's interests.

The first chapter of the book shows how you can access and use the wealth of language and literacy experiences that all children bring from their homes and communities to inform teaching and learning. This is closely followed by advice on how to motivate children for learning. Language is the driving force of our approach, specifically the languages that children use and the language that you use as part of your interaction with children. Concluding the first section with the chapter on assessment is perhaps misleading, as the importance of learning from observations and assessments of children is a strand that runs through the whole book.

The other parts of the book have both common and distinct elements. Both begin with the use of whole texts, suggest physical and social environments that are most likely to help children learn, and offer typical classroom strategies for teaching reading and writing effectively. As for distinct elements: in the reading section, the rich potential of children's names is highlighted (relatively insignificant to many adults, yet vital for children's learning). In the writing section, the final chapter covers handwriting, but this does not imply a lack of importance. In fact, you may be surprised to see one of our rare recommendations for decontextualised teaching!

At the time of writing, phonics teaching is once again high on the political agenda. If there is any political intent behind this book it is to stand firm, argue strongly for evidence and balance, and reclaim the curriculum and its pedagogy for you and your children. We hope you enjoy our book, and we hope it supports you in making a difference in children's lives.

---

4   Throughout the book when we refer to phonemes, we use the following format: /a/ (except in Table 12.1 in Chapter 12 where we use symbols from the international phonetic alphabet). When we refer to letter names we identify them like this: A. When referring to a letter we identify it like this: 'a'.

# Building on what children know

Sharing story books at home

Children should be at the centre of decisions made about teaching and learning. In order for this to happen, educators need to build on children's interests, experiences and understanding. However, it is too easy for what we might call child-centred education to be nothing but a truism; the practical reality takes sensitivity and rigour.

Child-centred learning is a much misunderstood idea, but a careful reading of the more thoughtful theorists reveals its relevance for modern educational environments. John Dewey, one of the leading thinkers in relation to child-centred education, argued that good teaching is built on the educator's understanding that there should be an interaction between educational aims and children's experiences and ideas. Less effective learning takes place if, instead of interaction, an opposition is built. Over-emphasis on transmission of facts to be learned from a formal

syllabus is one example of such opposition. Dewey was clear that the best knowledge available to society was the appropriate material for children's learning (hence it is untrue to imply that child-centred education is only about 'children teaching themselves'), but only through teaching that made a connection with children's experiences and thoughts. Dewey identified three "evils" of inappropriate curriculum material: a) material that is not organic to the child; b) material where the connecting links of need and aim are missing; c) lack of logical value.

To Dewey logical value was curriculum organisation that represented the best knowledge in society organised through a natural progression involving authentic hands-on experiences for the child. He said, "Guidance [by educators] is not external imposition. It is freeing the life-process for its own most adequate fulfilment"[1].

# BUILDING ON WHAT CHILDREN KNOW ·······························

Too often educators make assumptions about children's experiences and ideas. Consequently there can be a disparity between home settings and formal educational settings[2]. To a certain extent this disparity is natural as formal educational settings are, as the phrase makes clear, formal. But there is much that educators can do to recognise and build on children's home experiences. One aspect is a particular state of mind rather than direct action. This is an open mind about children's home experiences, an awareness that deficit models and low expectations of children impact negatively on learning[3], and a genuine interest in understanding the positive features of children's experiences out of school. This ability to search for and locate the positive in children's thinking should permeate work in classrooms as well as educators' reflections on children's lives outside formal education[4]. An important starting point for building on what children know is a genuine engagement with parents, both before and during their child's time in the setting. Although many parents may be reticent to share their knowledge with the educator who they will see as the 'expert', part of the skill of the educator is to encourage parents to do just that.

It is not only sensitivity and rigour in relation to understanding children's experiences outside formal education that is required. This also needs to be applied to understanding teaching and learning in the setting. Assuming that all has been done to positively assess children's understanding, there is a need to decide the experiences and learning that are most likely to help. An influential idea in relation to this is Lev Vygotsky's "zone of proximal development"[5]. In the course of his experiments Vygotsky discovered that a child who had a mental age of eight, as measured on a standardised test, was able to solve a test for a 12-year-old child if they were given "the first step in a solution, a leading question, or some other form of help" (Vygotsky, 1987, p 187). He suggested that the difference between the child's level working alone and the child's level with some assistance should be called the zone of proximal

development (ZPD). The idea of the ZPD suggests the need for educators to set activities based on prior assessments, then to interact with children in order to assess their development and use this information for the planning of further experiences.

If we accept the importance of the ZPD, it leaves a number of questions about how educator interaction can best support pupils' learning within it. The term 'scaffolding' has become commonplace in discussions about literacy teaching, as in the idea that educators should 'model' and scaffold aspects of writing. Unfortunately the didactic context for these recommendations is not the same as the original concept of 'scaffolding'. David Wood[6] used the term 'scaffolding' in his research on the teaching techniques that mothers used with their three- to four-year-old children. The mothers, who were able to help their children complete a task that could normally only be completed by children older than seven, scaffolded their children's learning in specific ways:

- They simplified problems that the child encountered

- They removed potential distractions from the central task

- They pointed things out that the child had missed.

The less successful parent tutors showed the child how to do the task without letting them have a go themselves or they used verbal instructions too much.

Overall, there were two particularly important aspects. When a child was struggling, immediate help was offered. Then, when help had been given, the mothers gradually removed support, encouraging the child's independence. "We termed this aspect of tutoring 'contingent' instruction. Such contingent support helps to ensure that the child is never left alone when he is in difficulty, nor is he 'held back' by

---

1   Dewey J (1902) *The Child and the Curriculum*. The University of Chicago Press, Chicago IL, USA, p 17.

2   Wells G (1986) *The Meaning Makers: Children learning language and using language to learn*. Hodder and Stoughton, London, UK. Marsh J (2003) One way traffic? Connections between literacy practices at home and in the nursery. *British Educational Research Journal*, 29(3), 370-382.

3   Mortimore P, Sammons P, Stoll L, Lewis D, Ecob R (1988) *School Years: The junior years*. Open Books Publishing Ltd, Wells, UK.

4   For an excellent example of positive reflections in the context of children's writing see Lessons from Latrice, a chapter in J C Harste, V A Woodward, C L Burke (1984) *Language Stories & Literacy Lessons*. Heinemann Educational Books, Portsmouth NH, USA.

5   Vygotsky L (Kozulin A, translator) (1987) *Thought and Language*. MIT Press, London, UK.

6   Wood D (1998) *How Children Think and Learn*. Second Edition. Blackwell, London, UK.

7   *Op cit.*, p 100.

···················································································································································

teaching that is too directive and intrusive."[7] The vital point here is that scaffolding happens in the context of meaningful interaction that is not inappropriately didactic.

## Engaging with parents' knowledge

Before a child starts at a setting educators begin the process of forming a mutually trusting relationship with the child's parents. This ideally starts with a home visit, because the home setting can put parents at ease and is a context where they are more likely to feel confident to express their knowledge about their child. There is also a benefit for educators because they have an opportunity to observe the child in an environment that is more familiar to them. The main purpose of the home visit is to provide the opportunity for everyone (the child, parents and educators) to get to know each other.

Figures 1.1 and 1.2 reveal the value of a home visit. Figure 1.1 is a record of a home visit made to Billy's house. The home visit record sheet provides a useful document to be built upon at the setting. Figure 1.2 is a record of an observation of Billy in the outside area of his early years setting. You can see how the educator uses the information from the home visit in discussion with the child and the child's parent during the child's early days in the nursery.

The week after the home visit Billy started nursery with his mother supporting him in the setting. John became his allocated keyworker (see Box 1.1). By the following week Billy was happy for his mother to leave him for one hour at a time. The setting had taken into account what the child's parents said at the home visit and built on the information that Billy had rarely been left anywhere by his mother.

### Box 1.1: Keyworker

Most early years settings allocate each child a keyworker. This means that the child and the child's parents have a person whom they can contact. Parents are able to approach the keyworker on a daily basis, especially in the early days when they want to know how their child is settling in. The keyworker organises the child's Record of Achievement and ensures that the child is benefiting from their early years experience. The keyworker will identify strengths and any concerns they may have regarding the child's development and learning and share these with the parents. Most importantly, they will share the child's successes and form a positive working partnership with the parents so that everyone is acting in the best interests of the child.

### Box 1.2: Record of Achievement (RoA)

A file that shows the child's interests and achievements in the setting. An RoA can be organised in a variety of ways. Most commonly it is organised by entries dated chronologically and sometimes divided into different areas of learning. The RoA includes a range of observations, photographs, and samples of the child's mark-making (drawing and writing).

# BUILDING ON WHAT CHILDREN KNOW ········································

**Figure 1.1: Home visit record made to provide information about the child's interests, the parents' concerns and to inform future nursery plans**

| | |
|---|---|
| **Child's name:** Billy Jones  **Child's age:** 3 years 1 month | **Date of visit:** 8th September 2010<br>**Time of visit:** 2.00pm to 2.30pm |
| **Child's parents' names:** Kate Jones and Simon Jones | **Educators:** Sue Webber, John Steele |

**Description**

We met Billy and both his parents. Billy is their first child; Kate is pregnant with their second child.

**What are your child's interests? What do they like to do most of all?**

Kate explained that Billy likes superheroes and often likes to wear his Spiderman outfit. Billy had asked whether he would be allowed to wear his outfit to nursery. It was explained that this wouldn't be a problem at all and that other children also liked to wear different outfits. On hearing this part of the conversation, Billy immediately went to his bedroom to find his Spiderman outfit to show us. He became a lot more animated and this was his prompt to show us other toys he had.

**Discussion about the opportunities for parents to share knowledge about their child**

Parents can:

● Look at child's Record of Achievement (see Box 1.2) at any time; it can also be taken home

● Share annotated photographs at times convenient to them

● Meet in a small group to talk informally about what their child has been doing at home and in the nursery.

**Other ways we could help?**

Kate and Simon expressed an interest in the Record of Achievement, but both felt they were too busy to join a group.

**How well do you think your child will settle into nursery?**

Kate said she is very anxious about Billy starting at nursery, although she does know it will be a positive experience for him. She explained that Billy spends most of his time with her and has rarely been away from her. She thought that seeing the observations and photographs would help her to adjust just as much as it would support Billy's learning.

**Do you have any other concerns or further information you haven't had an opportunity to tell us about?**

Simon voiced a concern that Billy is not interested in writing: he doesn't like to make marks at all. He is a very active child. They had heard from other parents that the children were expected to read and write.

John explained that Billy is still a young child, is doing what you would expect from a three year old and that it was good that he had so many opportunities to be active. Billy would have a full year in nursery before moving into the Reception class and still would not necessarily be expected to write in standard English. Play and talk would be an important focus to support mark-making, and because they are important in their own right. Billy's attention would also be drawn to the written word and adults would be modelling writing and reading within a range of supportive, relevant contexts.

John also explained that in the nursery they had several children starting with a keen interest in superhero play and the nursery team is planning to focus on this. This would include looking at different texts, such as *Super Daisy and the Peril of Planet Pea*[8].

---

8   Gray K, Sharrat N (2009) *Super Daisy and the Peril of Planet Pea*. Random House Children's Books, London, UK.

Figure 1.2: Child observation in an early years setting showing the link between the information from the home visit record and how Billy accesses the outdoor play area

| **Child's name:** Billy Jones **Child's age:** 3 years 2 months | **Date of observation:** 12th October 2010<br>**Time and length of observation:** 9.30am, 5 minutes |
|---|---|
| **Location:** Nursery garden | **Keyworker:** John Steele |

**Description**

9.30: Billy runs out and around the nursery garden at great speed. He is wearing his Spiderman outfit. He runs over the hill, along the concrete path, up to the trim trail [wooden structures for children to climb on] and balances along the log. He misses out the monkey bars, runs around the vegetable patch and then continues along the concrete path, around the corner and zigzags through the bamboo fence to the second smaller trim trail. He laughs as he runs across the swinging bridge and then returns to the start of his course. I observe him repeat this course three times.

9.40: The fourth time he slows down. When he is standing on the top of the hill he demonstrates his Spiderman actions, holding up each wrist in turn and he verbalises, "pisssssssssss". He repeats this action on top of one of the logs at the first trim trail and when he stands still on the wobbly bridge at the second trim trail. As he travels back to the start he pauses by the wooden house and peers in at the window. There are three children playing in there. He smiles and then runs away and shouts out, "I'm Spiderman, you can't catch me!"

**Note:** Photograph taken

**Reflections**

● Billy is able to select what he wants to do.

● Billy shows awareness of space around him. He doesn't bump into anything although he is travelling fast.

● He can run fast, climb with ease and confidence, jump off from a low height and demonstrates good balancing skills.

● He can create his own route around the nursery garden.

● Billy is showing a preference for lively solitary role play outside.

● Billy is beginning to show some awareness of the other nursery children.

**Next steps**

● Show Billy the photograph of his superhero outdoor play and encourage him to talk about what he was doing. Help Billy to stick the photograph into his Record of Achievement so that he knows where to find it.

● Show his parents this observation and the photograph. Emphasise how much Billy is enjoying the space provided in the nursery garden, how active he is and how he has already learnt to create a route around the garden.

● Continue to observe Billy's outdoor play and identify other times when he interacts with other children. Note any progress in his social development.

**Parent/s comment/s**

I am so happy that Billy has settled in so well. I love the photograph and I was so pleased that Billy wanted to show it to me himself. I pointed out to him that there is another child wearing a Spiderman outfit in the photograph and I asked him if he knew her name. He didn't, I think he might be brave, soon, to approach her, but I know not to push him.

By the way, his grandmother bought him a copy of *Super Daisy*, he hasn't stopped talking about it at home.

**CHAPTER 2** ·······················································

# Motivation for reading and writing

·················································································································

**Children motivated by play in a construction area**

One particularly important aspect of children's learning is their motivation. If children are motivated to learn, they are likely to learn better. There is a wide range of factors that contribute to motivation, but perhaps the most important idea is the difference between intrinsic and extrinsic motivation. Intrinsic motivation is motivation that comes from children's own curiosity, interests and preferences; extrinsic motivation comes from rewards that are external to the child, such as exam scores, formal assessments or physical rewards such as gold stars. Research evidence clearly shows that intrinsic motivation results in higher levels of learning than extrinsic motivation[1]. It has also been shown that classrooms which encourage intrinsic motivation are more likely to enhance children's creativity than those which emphasise extrinsic

motivation. Although it is difficult for educators to mitigate the negative effects of high stakes test regimes, even in these circumstances an emphasis on intrinsic motivation by educators can create an immunisation effect (*op cit.*) against the worst impacts of external systems.

A factor which contributes to children's motivation is the opportunity for play. The scenarios and resources which early years educators provide are important stimuli for children's play. When these are appropriate, most children become engaged and completely absorbed for extended periods of time. A broad and varied curriculum also contributes to children's motivation. The use of songs and music, outdoor play and explorations, imaginary worlds,

---

1   Hennessey B (2010) Intrinsic motivation and creativity in the classroom: Have we come full circle? In R Beghetto, J Kaufman (eds) *Nurturing Creativity in the Classroom.* Cambridge University Press, Cambridge, UK.

··············································································································

.......................... MOTIVATION FOR READING AND WRITING

**Reading the telephone directory in role play**

**Painting in the outdoor learning environment**

and hands-on physical experience, such as preparing and eating food, are just a few examples of the activities that can motivate children. Opportunities for choice over the curriculum motivate children powerfully. Early years settings have traditionally been very good at providing choice through play opportunities. However, choice is less frequent as children move up through the primary school, a trend that has been getting worse in recent years.

As far as the specifics of reading are concerned, research shows that there is a link between children's motivation and the amount and breadth of their reading[2]. Once again, intrinsic motivation has been found to be important as this is linked more strongly with amount and breadth than extrinsic motivation. The simple but powerful idea that the more reading children do, the better they become at it has also strong backing from research[3].

The texts that children read are also an important part of motivation for reading. The texts which motivate children the most are likely to be those created by real authors for the purpose of entertaining, informing, and provoking children to think in new ways. These books, called 'trade' books, are more likely to motivate than many books developed as skills training books, such as phonics training books, or poor examples from commercial reading schemes (or basals as they are called in the US). This is not to say that materials designed specially to support reading teaching do not have a place, it is just that educators must be discerning about the pros and cons of different texts.

Motivation for writing is rather more complex than for reading. In the earliest stages children enjoy mark-making, drawing and writing as part of their emergent literacy. But as children develop they come to understand how demanding writing is, both physically and cognitively. Writing is demanding for professional

2    Wigfield A, Guthrie J (1997) Relations of children's motivation for reading to the amount and breadth of their reading. *Journal of Educational Psychology*, 89(3), 420-432.

3    Stanovich K (1986) Matthew effects in reading: Some consequences of individual differences in the acquisition of literacy. *Reading Research Quarterly*, 21(4), 360-407.

# MOTIVATION FOR READING AND WRITING

writers and children alike. For many, these demands can be demotivating. Excessive focus on the mechanics of writing as opposed to a balanced focus can also be demotivating.

An approach to writing that proved to be very motivational is the process approach[4]. Although mainly applied in primary classrooms, elements of the process approach are often evident in exciting writing areas in early years settings. Other approaches that have been successful in motivating children for writing include: using drama as a stimulus; using experiences out of the classroom (see Chapter 3); generating writing from a variety of responses to children's literature; and book-making.

## Continuous provision and intrinsic motivation

Effective early years settings organise areas of provision which offer children opportunities to use carefully selected high quality resources in a well-organised and stimulating learning environment. This kind of organisation of the learning environment is often referred to as 'continuous provision' (see Box 2.1).

When children access the different areas of provision available to them, their keyworker becomes familiar with the range of the children's interests and what they are intrinsically motivated to do and to learn. Keyworkers identify those children who already read, make sense of print, enjoy looking at books, and notice print in the environment. They also identify those children for whom books, reading and making sense of print is an experience they are less familiar with.

Young children need to interact with adults who demonstrate a love of books and reading, who enthuse, and know which books children will be drawn to, both at home and in the early years setting. As well as introducing children to the world of literature, adults need to show the real purposes for reading, including the kind of reading that takes place outside the setting. For children to be motivated to read they need to be inspired to look at books independently as an individual, supported by an adult, and within a group. Walks out into

---

### Box 2.1: Continuous provision

Well-organised high quality resources in defined areas of the setting are available to the children daily, throughout the year. Young children become autonomous learners, knowing where everything is located and that they have the freedom to access what they need in order to follow their ideas and plans for their play. The areas of provision include: role play, sand, water, malleable materials, art (inclusive of painting, collage and modelling), small construction, small world, music, investigation, mark-making, writing, books, listening and computers. The outdoor learning area is also organised in areas of provision, for example role play, sand, water, large scale art, large scale construction, music, transport (including tricycles, bicycles and trolleys), transportable resources such as tools, playground chalk and pens (provided in work belts that fasten with Velcro) which can be used in the different areas, and large scale painting.

---

the community provide rich opportunities for showing young children print that we read in our daily lives.

Young children are eager to make marks. It is important to provide those opportunities in a range of areas in the setting as well as having defined writing and book-making areas. Not all children want to write at a table. Sometimes they might like to walk around with a clipboard, or to write in notebooks, on post-its, or on forms to fill in, re-enacting the adult world they observe daily. Outdoor opportunities could include use of decorators' paintbrushes. Adults will sometimes demonstrate writing in the different areas of provision, acting as role models to motivate children to write.

## Tessie's playing and learning

The following notes show how, from October to May, Tessie's literacy skills were developed through her play and learning in different areas of provision.

October: Tessie writes on a flipchart in the writing area all the letters she knows, using a large marker pen.

---

4   Wyse D (1998) *Primary Writing*. Open University Press, Buckingham, UK.

November: Tessie accesses the writing area to draw a picture of a visit to a soft play area with her family. She writes a caption for her story.

December: An educator notes that Tessie has chosen to look at Jill Murphy's *Whatever Next!*[5]. The story tells of when Baby Bear travels to the moon in a cardboard box that represents a rocket. Tessie asks the educator to read her the story. The educator reads, "Baby Bear was bored". Tessie explains, "That's because there is nobody on the moon. There is nothing there, nothing to play with". Having listened to the story, Tessie decides to fly to the moon herself and asks the educator for a cardboard box. She finds all the other props herself, a teddy bear, a jar of marmalade and an owl.

January: Tessie has enjoyed the story of the Gingerbread Man. She is self-motivated to access the writing area and write her version of the story, which she illustrates. Tessie uses her growing knowledge of phonics in her writing. She writes "jij man u kan me i jij bred man". Tessie says she has written, "Gingerbread man you can't catch me I'm gingerbread man".

February: Tessie is playing alongside three peers. Amy asks, "What new songs could we sing?" Tessie responds by singing out loud:

I like to eat, eat, eat!
Chicken and chips, chicken and chips, chicken and chips!
Ch, ch, ch, ch, ch!

March: Tessie has enjoyed the story, *Harry and the Bucketful of Dinosaurs*[6] in the book area. She suggests her own version to an adult, "Harry and his bucket of pencils!" Tessie laughs at her own joke.

May: The garden area has been enhanced with pots, compost, seeds, sticky labels and garden pencils. Tessie works with her friend Isabel. Together they put compost into several of the plant pots. Tessie and Isabel sow dill seeds. Tessie takes charge of writing the sticky labels for each plant pot. Isabel finds a piece of paper from inside to write a "Please do not touch" sign.

Tessie's play and learning was supported by the continuous provision educators planned including adult-initiated activities to further enhance and extend the children's literacy learning. These included a core story, the provision of writing materials as part of a new activity, and planned phonics sessions.

Drawing on the children's enthusiasm for rhymes and songs, many children's centres (providing for young children and their families from birth to four) have sessions that actively engage families in 'rhyme times' and 'interactive story times'. These sessions are mainly applicable to children in early years settings, but the development of children's love of rhyme and song is beneficial for older children too.

As children get older it is important to sustain their intrinsic motivation to read and write. This can be achieved by exploring literacy in the context of:

- Educational or library visits

- Visitors to the setting

- Planning to interview, for example, members of the school team, grandparents

- Visiting theatre groups

- ICT programmes

- Art projects

- Scientific investigations

- Drama role play

- Creating newsletters

- Writing to people of influence in the community, for example local councillors

- Musical performances.

---

5    Murphy J (2007) *Whatever Next!* Macmillan Children's Books, London, UK.

6    Whybrow I, Reynolds A (1999) *Harry and the Bucketful of Dinosaurs*. Puffin Books, London, UK.

# MOTIVATION FOR READING AND WRITING

## Rhyme time

The purpose of rhyme time is to engage parents and children in developing orally a repertoire of songs and rhymes. Songs and rhymes frequently include actions. We know young children respond very well to songs and rhymes involving physical interaction.

## A rhyme time session

As the children arrive with their parents the educator plays a CD, *Asian Dreamland*[7], to create a calm atmosphere. Everyone sits in a circle. The educator introduces the first song, *Hello Everybody*, which is sung to the tune of Skip to My Lou[8].

Hello everybody, how are you?
Hello everybody, how are you?
Hello everybody, how are you?
How are you today?
Hello Lisa, how are you?
Hello Harry, how are you?
Hello Jamaal, how are you?
How are you today?

For the second rhyme the educator selects *Ten Little Monkeys*[9], a rhyme the children know well and are confident to participate in. Counting up and counting down are popular features in rhymes.

Ten little monkeys jumping on the bed,
One fell off and bumped his head,
Mama sent for doctor, the doctor said,
No more monkeys jumping on the bed!

Nine little monkeys ...

To introduce the third rhyme, the educator uses a soft toy banana as a prop. It is a new rhyme for the children, *Bananas!*[10]

Bananas, Bananas, clap, clap, clap!
*(Clap hands)*
Bananas, Bananas, tap, tap, tap!
*(Tap knees)*
Bananas, Bananas, click, click, click!
*(Click fingers)*
Bananas, Bananas, flick, flick, flick!
*(Flick fingers out)*
Bananas, Bananas, bump, bump, bump!
*(Bump up and down)*
Bananas, Bananas, jump, jump, jump!
*(Jump up and down)*

For the fourth rhyme, the educator provides a pompom for every child and every adult. This song is sung to the tune of Polly Put the Kettle On.

Can you shake your pompom?
Can you shake your pompom?
Can you shake your pompom?
Just like this!

Other verses can be made up, for example:

Can you shake it in the air?

The next rhyme is *The Grand Old Duke of York*[11]. The children and adults use the pompoms to exaggerate the movements in the song.

Oh the grand old Duke of York, he had ten thousand men,
He marched them up to the top of the hill
*(Shake pompoms up in the air)*
And he marched them down again
*(Shake pompoms low down on the ground)*
And when they were up they were up
*(Shake pompoms up in the air)*
And when they were down they were down
*(Shake pompoms low down)*

---

7  Putumayo Kids (2006) *Asian Dreamland*. Putumayo World Music, New York, USA (available from www.putumayokids.com).

8  Harrop B (ed) (2001) *Hey Diddle Diddle*. A&C Black, London, UK.

9  Freeman T (illustrator) (2001) *Ten Little Monkeys Jumping on the Bed*. Child's Play (International) Ltd.

10  Mclavish A (2008) Bananas! In *Sing a Song, Tell a Tale. Enriching children's experience through music, drama and movement*. Early Education, London, UK.

11  Harrop B (ed) (2001) The Grand Old Duke of York. In *Hey Diddle Diddle*. A&C Black, London, UK.

And when they were only half way up
*(Shake pompoms in front)*
They were neither up nor down.
*(Shake pompoms up and down)*

To finish rhyme time, the educator introduces the *Goodbye Song* (sung to Skip to My Lou[8]).

Goodbye everybody, it's time to go
Goodbye everybody, it's time to go
Goodbye everybody, it's time to go
See you again next week!

As the children and their parents leave the session, the educator puts the calming CD back on.

These songs and rhymes, which have been successfully developed by early years educators, demonstrate how any song or rhyme that captures either your imagination or that of the children has the potential to be further developed to extend the children's learning.

## Interactive story time

The purpose of interactive story time for the youngest children is to engage the child, parents and carers in enjoying a range of different stories. Stories need to be presented to children and adults with and without props, with and without a text.

To engage the youngest children in looking at a book, there are many books that are baby friendly and encourage adult and baby to be actively involved in enjoying the text. All babies love the game of peekaboo. In *Noisy Peekaboo Splash! Splash!*[12] we see five different babies all looking for a toy they want at bath time. This is a photograph book and each part of the story has three flaps to lift. The third flap includes the sound of the toy. There is a repeated pattern to the text, including repeated questions, inviting the young child's engagement. For example:

Baby can't find Splashy Fish.
Where is Splashy Fish hiding?

Let's look! Where can he be?
Is he behind the little watering can?
Is he behind the stacking cups?
Is he under the big fishing nets?

The following example demonstrates how the educator uses props to tell a story and keeps the storytelling flexible to adapt according to the children in the group.

The educator introduces a soft toy kitten. She explains that the kitten went shopping.

"Let's see what Katy Kitten has bought. Here's her basket."
*(The educator takes each item out of the basket slowly)*

"There's a tin of beans, some carrots. Let's count the carrots, 1, 2, 3, 4! There's a packet of pasta, a bag of rice, a jar of marmalade and a loaf of bread."

"Oh look! What's this? A present! It looks like a birthday present. Can anyone guess what it is?"
*(The educator passes the present round, letting every child touch and feel the present and guess what it is)*

"We'll put everything back now. Can you remember what Katy Kitten had in her basket?"

Another example of a text that works well for interactive story time is *The Very Busy Bee*[13]. Minibeasts are introduced on each double page spread: bee, ant, earthworm, dragonfly, snail, grasshopper, dung beetle and caterpillar. A wonderful pop up creature jumps out of the page. Movement and sound words are emphasised, such as "Wriggle! Wriggle!" for the earthworms and "Boing! Boing!" for the grasshopper. These books can be used to motivate children to move.

It is important to repeat those stories that are particularly popular with the young children and their parents. This is not always predictable; what one group loves, another may reject. What is important is to make sure the session is full of fun so the children are more likely to develop an intrinsic love of stories and books.

---

12  Sirett D (2009) *Noisy Peekaboo Splash! Splash!* Dorling Kindersley, London, UK.

13  Tickle J (2008) *The Very Busy Bee.* Little Tiger Press, London, UK.

# High quality literacy teaching

***The Twelve Dancing Princesses*** inspires children's play and literacy learning

High quality literacy teaching ensures that the teaching of smaller units, such as phonemes, syllables, words and sentences, is contextualised in complete or whole texts. This enables children to understand the connections at different levels of language. In this chapter we focus on reading and writing separately because the decoding and comprehension required for reading are distinct from the encoding and composition required for writing. The main difference between decoding and encoding is that encoding is a more active process which requires the writer to develop ideas and then formulate them in appropriate words and sentences. Decoding, on the other hand, requires an understanding of the alphabetic code so the reader can access meaning and comprehend basic and complex ideas. Although reading and writing have distinct processes, they are also interconnected.

## Reading

Reading is the process of understanding speech written down. The goal is to gain access to meaning.[1]

One straightforward way to ensure contextualised teaching of reading is to begin a lesson or sequence of teaching with a complete text. Sometimes the text will be new to the children, at other times it will be well known. In the early stages of learning to read it is important that children frequently encounter texts that they know. Each encounter allows for something new to be discovered and taught. The repetition of language that comes from regular readings also enables children to memorise parts of the text, something that contributes to their

---

1   Ziegler J, Goswami U (2005) Reading acquisition, developmental dyslexia and skilled reading across languages: A psycholinguistic grain size theory. *Psychological Bulletin*, 131(1), 3-29.

**Educators use puppets to engage and motivate children**

Once a text is familiar to children, then the focus on linguistic units below the level of the whole text (words, letters and sounds) is more meaningful (see Box 3.1 on the importance of using appropriate terminology for such teaching). This is where the opportunity for the whole group to see the same text is so useful. A visualiser (or document camera) is one of the most useful tools for this, although big books and texts downloaded to interactive whiteboards can be used as well.

## Writing

If access to meaning is the key to reading, then communication of meaning is the driving force for writing. At the socio-cultural level children need to understand that writing is done for a particular purpose and with particular readers in mind. Educators quite rightly set up contexts for writing that reflect real life processes. Sometimes these involve writing to real people to communicate a particular message; at other times fictional scenarios are created in order to engage children. A memorable example from a school in Scotland was the creation of Mr Togs the Tailor and his shop in the classroom which emerged from what began as a topic on clothing[2]. As with reading, children need to be motivated for the much harder challenge which writing represents. This requires your enthusiasm about writing and its development and positive feedback for children's successes and things of interest. Authentic writing tasks are more effective than photocopied worksheets or pupil text books from published schemes. The main reason for this is that if the educator plans the learning, then the tasks are based on their direct assessment of the pupils they are teaching. If a published resource is used, it is more difficult to match the learning intentions of the resource with the needs of the children. A second reason is that good teaching has clear aims but is also responsive to children's emerging needs. It is often much more difficult, if not impossible, to be responsive when following the steps of a pupil book or published worksheet.

development as readers. For older children the introduction of new texts that interest and challenge them is the priority although the enjoyment of old favourites is also valuable.

If the text is new to children, then the first reading provides an opportunity for a dramatic, uninterrupted story reading. There are few things so magical in teaching as the rapt expressions of a class of children deeply engaged with a story. The first reading also gives the opportunity to have a brief conversation with the children about the wider socio-cultural context of books, such as considering who the author is and their background. Most importantly there needs to be discussion about the meanings of the text after the first complete story reading has taken place. Literal meanings (such as the name of a character or key events in a story) are a natural starting point because without these the inferential meanings (such as a character's motivation for doing something that is not made explicit) cannot be grasped.

The best approach to writing is to encourage children to do as much as they can themselves and provide just enough support. For example, educators can encourage children's mark-making in a classroom writing area, then engage with

2    Committee on Primary Education (1982) *Mr Togs the Tailor: A context for writing.* The Scottish Curriculum Development Service, Edinburgh, UK.

# HIGH QUALITY LITERACY TEACHING

individual children by praising specific aspects of their writing (particularly the meanings ascribed by the child) and then suggesting the ways in which improvements could be made, often by comparing with a standard English version of the writing scribed by the educator. Mark-makers are any tool you can make a mark with, for example pens, pencils, felt pens and chalk as well as hand and finger prints in paint and the footprints you make when you walk through a puddle.

Writing needs to be seen as a process, not a one-off event. The processes of writing are planning, drafting, editing and proofreading. For young children these processes are in embryonic forms, but for older children they become more explicitly understood. Early forms of planning include brainstorming, or talking to a partner about things to write about, or using role play as a way into writing. Embryonic forms of drafting include the educator helping the child think about changes they could make to the meaning of their writing, even if the child's writing is mark-making and not in a conventional form. Helping children to see writing as a process is supported by a clear focus on teaching about strategies for writing[3]. The process of making books, individual children's books and books made from group contributions, is an invaluable way of exploring all the processes of writing from generating ideas to final presentation skills.

Other areas of writing, such as handwriting and spelling, are also vital. Children need to make good progress in these areas not only as skills in their own right, but because their ability to compose writing will improve.

## Reading – four year olds

Reading sessions for four year olds are usually 10 to 15 minutes long. Adult-directed sessions are supported by the continuous provision of resources and activities in the different areas of the early years setting. These areas provide opportunities to further extend themes of work, for example through role play including small world play.

> ### Box 3.1: Using appropriate terminology
>
> It is important for educators to use appropriate terminology with children. The word 'phoneme' should be used because it has a distinct meaning from 'sound'. The names of letters should be used to refer to letters not common phonemes, e.g. 'letter A' not 'letter /a/'.

The educator selects one text as a main focus for two weeks. Usually this is a classic children's picture book which will motivate the children because of the quality of the text and its illustrations and the educator's enthusiasm for the story. Texts which children can naturally join in with are often used. Children learning to engage with texts benefit from hearing stories repeated. The educator's aim is for the children to enjoy the oral aspect of storytelling, as well as relating what they hear to what they see.

In *Brown Bear, Brown Bear, What do you See?*[4] the book begins with Brown Bear being asked the question, "What do you see?" Each of the other characters who is asked the same question is an animal described by a colour, for example "red bird", "purple cat". At the end of the story the last character says, "I see children looking at me!"

To introduce this story, the educator can use a bear puppet to capture the children's interest prior to the first session. Before the story starts the children ask the bear puppet questions about, for example, where he lives and what he eats. The educator asks the puppet, "Brown Bear, Brown Bear, what do you see?" and the bear puppet answers, "I see a red bird looking at me". The educator tells the rest of the story and makes the bear puppet show it is listening by looking at the different animals that are projected on the interactive whiteboard. The children discuss with their talk partners (see Box 3.2) the names of the animals and any facts they already know.

Each reading session lasts for approximately 10 minutes. This is appropriate for four-year-old children and also means that the children's interest and motivation are maintained. However, it is

---

3    Graham S (2010) Facilitating writing development. In D Wyse, R Andrews, J Hoffman (eds) *The Routledge International Handbook of English, Language and Literacy Teaching.* Routledge, London, UK.

4    Martin B Jnr (Carle E, illustrator) (1967) *Brown Bear, Brown Bear, What do you See?* Henry Holt and Company, New York, USA.

essential that the learning from the reading session is revisited as part of the children's independent play and learning. To further engage the children in the story the educator provides:

- A copy of the story in the book area

- Animals from the book in the small world area

- Colour words (related to the colours of the animals) in the art area, accompanying a display of postcards depicting the work of artists

- Laminated photographs of the animals shown on the interactive whiteboard and corresponding animal names in the writing area.

The teaching staff respond to children's interests with the aim of consolidating their understanding of the text. For example, a group of children is keen to play with the animals in the small world area. The adult observes the children's play and prompts them by referring to the text if they have difficulty remembering the sequence of animals in the story. The children respond to the educator's interest in their play by maintaining concentration for an extended period of time. The children start to create their own stories about the animals through their play and then the adult scribes their spoken words.

## A favourite picture book – session one

Before reading the story the educator has a quick reminder discussion, for example checking that the children are familiar with the names of the animals in the story. The educator tells the story orally, using the bear puppet and the animal images on the interactive whiteboard. Then the story is read to the children. The children are invited to recall the sequence of animals that appears in the story.

## A favourite picture book – session two

The educator does a quick reminder of the previous reading session and retells the story. She explains that this lesson has a new focus on some of the sentences and words in the story. The children already have some understanding of

> ### Box 3.2: Talk partners
>
> The children have a 'talk partner' who they sit next to during taught sessions. The educator assigns the talk partners so that all children benefit from the child they are paired with. It is good practice to change talk partners during the year so that children gain from working with different children. The purpose of having a talk partner is that all the children have the opportunity to talk about what they are learning during the taught part. They are not always passively listening, they are actively learning by discussing what they are learning.

phonemes and diagraphs, but they are still learning how to apply their phonic knowledge to decode texts. They need time to play with words and texts so that they become more familiar, and they need adults to demonstrate segmentation and blending within a context with which they are confident.

**Educator:** Brown Bear, Brown Bear, what do you see?

**Educator and children:** Brown Bear, Brown Bear, what do you see?

**Educator:** What other words do we know with the phoneme /ow/ in 'Brown'?

The educator has a colourful box of objects which demonstrate the /ow/ phoneme. These objects include: a doll dressed in a 'ball-gown'; a cow; a ladder to illustrate 'down'; a sow (pig). The objects are passed around so that the children have the opportunity to become familiar with them. Next, two games are played: Shake the Bag and Countdown.

### Shake the Bag

The educator has a cloth drawstring bag which contains the objects that demonstrate the phoneme /ow/ and laminated cards with the corresponding words to match the objects. The following rhyme is sung to the tune of Skip to My Lou. One child is chosen to select a word and read it out to the group.

Shake, shake, shake the bag
Shake, shake, shake the bag
Shake, shake, shake the bag
Can you read the word?

# HIGH QUALITY LITERACY TEACHING ·······································

## Countdown

The four /ow/ words are written as a list on the flipchart. Together the children sound out and read each word. The educator leads the group and an assistant times the children (on other occasions the roles can be reversed). The class has three goes to see if they can speed up each time.

The objects and laminated words are made available for the children to play with during independent play and learning. A one minute timer is also provided for children to practise their sounding out and reading. The educator encourages the children to engage with the resources during their play. Sometimes a record of the children's achievements and next steps is made. For example, the educator might record when a child is able to read the words; use the words in a meaningful context; use the laminated words to write independently; or correct letter formation and left to right orientation.

## A favourite picture book – session three

The educator retells the story. The children play the Shake the Bag game. Most children have had an opportunity to revisit the game during their play so their confidence has increased, something they are eager to show. For this session the focus is on the sentence, "What do you see?" and the phoneme /ee/. The educator also draws the children's attention to the question mark.

The educator leads a game of What do you See?

**Children:** Miss Richards, Miss Richards, what do you see?

**Educator:** I see Joanne looking at me.

**Children:** Joanne, Joanne, what do you see?

**Joanne:** I see Ali looking at me.

**Educator:** Class 1, Class 1, what do you see?

**Children:** We see Miss Richards looking at us!

**Educator:** What words do we know that have the /ee/ phoneme?

The children share their ideas and the educator scribes their words on the board.

The educator has objects to demonstrate the phoneme /ee/: a finger puppet bumble bee, a packet of seeds, a soft toy with big feet, and a beetroot. The Shake the Bag game is played again, but this time with different objects and words. Scaffolding is provided by the structure of the game, but new learning comes from the new objects and words. The children participate with increasing enthusiasm because they know the game. The Countdown game is also played again with different words. For the more experienced children the game is played with all eight words.

To end the session the educator revisits the story *Brown Bear, Brown Bear, What do you See?*, re-introducing the bear puppet from the first session. The children are now so familiar with the text they are able to join in with enthusiasm and a sense of achievement. Some children are keen to read the text independently.

## A favourite picture book – session four

Before the educator retells the story she begins by asking the children if they can read any of the words. The children are given a few minutes' discussion with their talk partner to decide whether they can recall any of the words. A more confident child is invited to demonstrate to the whole group the words they know and to segment and blend.

The game What do you See? is played again. This time the focus is on the response sentence, "I see ... looking at me". The educator plays the game with an assistant to demonstrate how the children can play this game in pairs. The children enjoy the demonstration and are excited about having a turn themselves with their talk partner. The adults support the pairs of children who they know may struggle. The educator invites some pairs of children to show the whole group how they have played the game.

All educators working with the children know to initiate the game during the day for further reinforcement and extension. The aim is for children to become so confident that they are able to play with the words of the question and the response.

## A favourite picture book – session five

The educator revisits the game What do you See? The children are asked to think of other words they know ending in 'ing' and are given a few minutes to talk to their talk partner. An assistant participates to give extra support to some children and to record the children's ideas on the flipchart. The educator anticipates that many of the words will be familiar actions.

> **Educator:** Let's practise these actions outside [or in the school hall]!

The children enjoy the physical activity and are keen to practise running, jumping, skipping, hopping and turning. While they are engaged in this activity, another adult takes photographs which will either be projected onto the interactive whiteboard during the day for discussion, or printed off, laminated and displayed. There is space in front of the whiteboard to enable small groups of children to imitate the action they see in the photograph.

The children become so familiar with the text that they are then ready for book-making based on that story (see Chapter 14 for examples of this kind of writing).

One morning parents are invited in to share books with their own child. Six copies of Brown Bear, Brown Bear, What do you See? are provided so that the children can inform their own parent or carer about the text and what they know. The children also share the books they have made and their own versions of the story.

## Reading – six year olds

The class has been focussing on the story The Rainbow Fish[5]. The educator decides to change to using non-fiction texts. The children's reading development is at different stages so the educator selects three texts that enable all the children to engage. The selected texts are Snappy Sharks[6],

### Aims for reading sessions with four year olds

**Teaching aims**

● Encourage children's enthusiasm for a text.

● Ensure children know the meaning(s) of the text.

● Develop children's vocabulary and ability to read words in the text.

**Assessment evidence in children's language**

● "I can read Brown Bear, Brown Bear!"

● "I can read these words!"

● "I can play Countdown and I am getting faster in my reading!"

Under the Sea[7] and Freaky Fish[8]. Although texts are provided at three levels of differentiation, the educator is happy for children to attempt texts which may be too difficult, and not to assume that children who need the most support should not be challenged by being exposed to the harder texts.

A tropical fish theme is launched by visiting a large pet shop with aquariums on display. The children closely observe the fish and this visit generates many questions. The educator also plans an educational visit to the seaside, including a trip to a Sealife Centre. This use of experiences from outside the classroom is one of the ways in which the educator ensures that reading teaching is contextualised in real life experiences that the children can relate to. Children's learning is strengthened when there is a direct correlation to personal experiences, especially those shared with their peer group and educators[9]. The educator plans class activities (whole

5   Pfister M (1992) The Rainbow Fish. NorthSouth Books, New York, USA.

6   Owen R (2009) Snappy Sharks. Ticktock Media Ltd, Tunbridge Wells, UK.

7   Patchett F (2002) Under the Sea. Usborne Publishing Ltd, London, UK.

8   Burns R (2003) Freaky Fish. Oxford University Press, Oxford, UK.

9   Dewey J (1902) The Child and the Curriculum. The University of Chicago Press, Chicago IL, USA.

# HIGH QUALITY LITERACY TEACHING ·······················

class and small group) to further embed the meaning of the texts and to ensure that the children consolidate the benefits of the educational visit.

## Non-fiction – session one

Before the children move into their guided reading groups (see Box 3.3) the educator reminds them all about their visit to the pet shop and the tropical fish they saw there. The children discuss the photographs of their visit that are projected onto the interactive whiteboard. For two minutes they talk to their talk partners about the different fish they observed.

In *Freaky Fish* different fish are described including their appearance, their habitats, what they eat and their special features. Some of the fish included are the porcupinefish, the treefish and the lionfish. One of the educator's intentions is for the children to become familiar with words related to their theme prior to the visit to the Sealife Centre.

In their guided reading group the children look through the book and each chooses one fish to draw and write a sentence about. They have time to flick through and decide what particularly attracts their attention. In their sentences they comment on camouflage, how the fish wards off enemies, and the reason they have selected that fish to draw. This activity familiarises the children with the text before reading through the book in more detail.

Every day children work in small groups to develop their reading skills. Each child in the group has a copy of the book. Sometimes they work independently and at other times an adult will support them. Each reading group has a different plan to ensure they have an appropriate level of work and they can complete the task as a collaborative group.

## Non-fiction – session two

The children are eager to read *Freaky Fish* together. Some tell the educator, who is focussing on their group for this session, that they like it so much they had already read some of it. In this second session the children are using the text to find out information. The educator provides a questions dice. The children roll the dice, and the educator asks the appropriate question. As the children become more confident, the educator takes on the role of the learner and each child has a turn as the educator. As children answer the different questions, they are expected to locate where they found the answer, providing the correct page number for the group.

Some of the questions are:

- What does the word 'camouflage' mean?
- Which part of the text tells how fish warn off their enemies?
- Why does the porcupinefish blow up like a balloon?
- How does the stargazer hide from its enemies?
- What does the trumpet fish eat?
- When does the treefish hunt for food?
- Where do sarcastic fringeheads [yes this really is the name of a fish!] live?

Having played the Question game, the children are ready to recall the facts they have found out. Working in their talk partners they write quick notes to remind themselves of the knowledge they have acquired. The educator then asks for a different fact from each talk pair until the children have run out of answers.

## Non-fiction – session three

The children are now more familiar with the text and they return to their favourite fish which they wrote about and illustrated in the first session. The educator invites them to prepare a short oral presentation about their favourite fish for the rest of the class. The presentation is to include their reasons for selection. The children work in pairs and have to agree on one fish. They know they have time the next day to focus on their presentation

> ### Box 3.3: Guided reading
>
> Guided reading involves an educator working with a small group of pupils who each have a copy of the same text or are all able to see the same text. The pupils are selected so that they have similar attainment levels.

skills, so they are able to spend time planning, reasoning and negotiating. The children work without adult support and have had previous experience of working in this way. They can use a presentation structure if needed (see Figure 3.1).

## Non-fiction – session four

The educator checks that the children are able to finish their presentations. The children are provided with space and time to practise their presentations.

### Aims for reading sessions with six year olds

#### Teaching aims

- Children are eager to engage in non-fiction texts.

- Children identify accurate information they did not know before.

- Children can decide what they enjoy most about a text and why.

- Children can communicate what they enjoy about a text, for example through oral presentations and by writing book reviews.

#### Assessment evidence in children's language

- "Isn't the fish in that book amazing?"

- "I didn't think that sarcastic fringehead was a real fish name at first."

- "I can read these difficult words because I have seen these fish in the pet shop. I remember them and what they are called."

- "I told the whole class about my favourite fish. I was brave and used a loud voice."

- "My book review shows I know something about *Freaky Fish*. It will be printed in the school newsletter!"

---

**Freaky Fish**

My Favourite Fish

**Presentation Plan**

Name ...Mubik...Akram......

Date ..14.12.2011..

*Introduction*

The purpose of this presentation is to ......talk and.... Write about My Favourite Fish...............

*Middle Section*

We have chosen the ......Porcupine....Fish..... because ......It has Spikes on its body.......

*Final Section*

We recommend Freaky Fish because ....there are..... Intresting facks about the fish.........

Thank you for listening.

**Figure 3.1: A presentation structure**

---

**Book Review**

**Title:** ......Freaky Fish..........
**Author:** ...Maana Ashley...........

What is this non-fiction book about?

It is about different type of fish.

What is the most interesting piece of information you have found out? I have found out that fish can contained...

What would make this book better? ...add more fish and creatures...

Explain why you would recommend this to your friend ...To Learn about different kinds of fish and what they are like.

**Figure 3.2: A review structure**

# HIGH QUALITY LITERACY TEACHING ......................................

At the end of the session each of the four pairs presents to the whole class. The children watching and listening are encouraged to identify the positive features of the presentations and make recommendations for improvement.

## Non-fiction – session five

In the last session working on the text *Freaky Fish* the children consider what they liked about the book and whether they would recommend it to their friends. The children have access to a book review writing frame (see Figure 3.2), but the educator encourages them to write independently without the frame if possible. The children know that some of their reviews will be used for the school's newsletter for children. This provides a real audience for the reviews. Within the group of eight some children decide to work independently and others work in pairs. The educator encourages the children to make such decisions for themselves.

## Writing – four year olds

As we suggested in Chapter 1, it is important to build on children's enthusiasms. For example children's interest in superheroes can feed into role play and writing. An early years team did just this by creating a role play story that involved a fictional character, Nick the Napper. The team set the context of the head teacher being kidnapped by Nick the Napper (with this role played by a member of the team). The children receive a letter from Nick the Napper containing the first clue of a trail to help them rescue the head teacher. (See Box 3.4 on the importance of treating topics like kidnapping with sensitivity.) Making 'wanted' posters to help them catch Nick the Napper is the first writing activity.

## A 'wanted' poster – session one

Photographs taken of the kidnapping and of the class following the clues are projected onto the interactive whiteboard. The educator discusses the events of the morning with the children. They are shown a 'wanted' poster and the educator focusses on the letter 'w'. The children discuss other words they know beginning with 'w' with their talk partners. A teaching assistant scribes the words on the flipchart as the children feed back to the whole group. The educator returns to the word 'wanted'. The bilingual teaching assistant translates and explains the meaning of 'wanted' for any bilingual children who need this support.

Two children are chosen to distribute individual whiteboards and pens, ready for the children to practise writing the letter 'w'. The educator demonstrates writing 'w' on the flipchart for the children who remain on the carpet. The children write for themselves on their individual whiteboards. Some children are encouraged to write zigzag lines to develop flow and confidence. The educator provides differentiation for those children whose writing is at an earlier stage of development. For example, a small group goes outside to practise writing 'w' using large paintbrushes and water on the playground and fence.

The educator has prepared a writing frame for the 'wanted' poster which is available for the children should they need it.

For the children's independent play and learning, the educators have provided the following in the areas of continuous provision:

- 'Wanted' poster writing frames in the mark-making area

- 'Wanted' poster writing frames on the outdoor play trolley, alongside the mark-makers and clipboards

- A collection of objects beginning with 'w' for children to play Feely Bag and I Spy games: wheels (from any toy

### Box 3.4: Sensitivity about topics

The team was mindful that a minority of children might be worried by the kidnapper scenario. They ensured that the children understood it was a 'pretend' role play. They also informed the children's families in their weekly newsletter and verbally reassured the parents. Having an open mind towards sensitive topics can provide the opportunity for children to talk about their fears. There are times when these need to be shared with the child's parents.

**Nick the Napper**

**Figure 3.3: A sample 'wanted' poster**

vehicle); a Duplo window; a wig from the dressing-up trolley; a superhero watch; a finger puppet worm

- In the construction area laminated pictures of vehicles have been provided to support children to make models. This supports children's conversations about what begins with 'w'.

## A 'wanted' poster – session two

The photos are revisited and discussed again. The children are encouraged to retell the story of the kidnapping using full sentences. The educator helps the children to extend their oral vocabulary. Some of the 'wanted' posters from the first session are shown to the whole class (see Figure 3.3).

The focus for the second session is writing names: the children's own names; friends' names; adults' names; and the all-important name of Nick the Napper! (See Chapter 9 for more on the importance of children's names.) The children write their own names on the individual whiteboards and

discuss them with their talk partner. Everyone's achievements are acknowledged, and additional support is given to those children who are more reluctant and less experienced. Children who are confident in writing their own name are then asked to write their friends' names. Their names are visible in the classroom, for example on the children's trays, name cards used for registration, and name cards used in the mark-making area. Finally the educator demonstrates writing "Nick the Napper". This remains visible on the flipchart so that children can check their attempts at independent writing.

The additional resources provided for the first session remain, and the following additional opportunities are offered:

- Games with tally charts are set up outside, such as skittles, with the children's name cards available

- The children are invited to write their names on a large piece of chart paper after they have finished their snack

- In the home corner blank birthday party invitations encourage the children to write names.

# HIGH QUALITY LITERACY TEACHING

## A 'wanted' poster – session three

The educator leads a quick reminder discussion about the Nick the Napper episode and the reason why they are making the 'wanted' posters. The children learn that their parents have been talking about the kidnapping. The educator has managed to make a note of what some parents have told her and shows the children that she has put this up on a 'learning at home' display board.

The educator focusses on the writing the children have achieved in independent writing. The children share the different names they have written on paper. The group also looks at the names that children have written on the children's display board.

The educator models writing a 'Wanted: Nick the Napper' poster on paper and the children are now eager to have a go themselves. One educator takes a small group of less experienced children to the art area, where there are large pieces of paper for the children to write and illustrate their posters. The writing frame is provided to give individual children the support they need to get started.

The more experienced children have already made their posters. They are now working on an account of the kidnapping to accompany the series of Nick the Napper photographs. The photographs were shown to all the children at the beginning of the first session. This group works on the account with another educator, ready to share with the class the next day.

## A 'wanted' poster – session four

To begin the session the educator shows some of the finished 'wanted' posters and explains that they need to be displayed around the school. Not every child has finished their poster, but they know that they will have time and that adult support will be provided during independent play and learning time to enable them to finish their poster. The children who have written their own account to accompany the photographs share what they have done. The educator projects the images onto the interactive whiteboard as the children read their writing. The class is informed that copies of the photographic storyboard are available in the

### Aims for writing sessions with four year olds

Teaching aims

- Engage children in a role play scenario performed by the early years team.

- Develop the children's understanding of posters.

- Develop children's writing of their own name, other names, and "Nick the Napper".

- Learn to write the letter 'w'.

Assessment evidence in children's language

- "I know this is a story. It's not real."

- "I am learning to write the letter 'w'."

- "I am getting better at writing my name."

- "I can write my friend's name."

- "I can write 'Nick the Napper'."

- "I can make my own 'wanted' poster."

mark-making area and that they can all have a go at writing their own accounts. The educators know that the children will approach this at different levels. During independent play and learning small groups of children are taken by an educator to display their finished posters around the school.

## A 'wanted' poster – session five

The educators have arranged for a group of children from Key Stage 2 to come to the class and tell the children that they have seen their posters and have some important information. A person matching the description of Nick the Napper has been seen in various places around the school. The older children have prepared a map for the Foundation Stage children to follow.

**A visit photograph inspires a child's writing**

**The Castle Rising display of art work**

Everyone sets off to follow the map and eventually they find Nick the Napper in the playhouse outside. The educator playing Nick the Napper apologises for what happened and explains that he went to the police station to give himself in. Nick has now decided to be a superhero and help people. The children are shown his new superhero outfit and are asked how they could all be more helpful.

## Writing – six year olds

A good way to contextualise writing for children is through creating a theme for the work. The following work on writing used castles as a theme. The theme was selected for three main reasons. Firstly, the children had shown an interest in castles when engaged in small world play. They had built a castle out of wooden bricks and then used the fairy tale figures to make up their own stories. The children's interest in castles also included depictions in books and films;

they enjoyed singing the song *There Was a Princess Long Ago*[10], building castles outside, and participating in role play. Secondly, the educator knew a nearby castle which could be visited. Thirdly, the educator thought the visit and the theme would motivate the children.

Outdoor learning environments are often exciting for children. A trip to Castle Rising in Norfolk was no exception! Prior to the visit the educator led circle times for children to consider what they wanted to find out about the castle, what they thought they would see and to introduce and reinforce key vocabulary such as 'moat', 'keep', 'mound' and 'portcullis'.

### A trip to Castle Rising – introductory session

The educator wanted to rekindle the enthusiasm the children had shown during the trip so she encouraged lots of talk to start with:

---

10  Harrop B (ed) (1976; current edition 2010) *Okki-tokki-unga*. A&C Black, London, UK.

# HIGH QUALITY LITERACY TEACHING

- Photos taken while on the trip were shown on the interactive whiteboard. Children were encouraged to talk about these with a talk partner.

- The educator had a two minute brainstorm of good words to use for the writing. The children suggested 'Castle Rising', 'coach', 'arrived', 'archway', 'moat', 'portcullis'. She also added some words of her own to extend the children's vocabulary, such as 'travelled', 'afterwards', 'observed', 'mound', 'finally'.

- Children were encouraged to put labels with arrows on the interactive whiteboard photos.

- The educator acted as scribe to write a few example beginning sentences using the children's ideas. She wrote phrases such as "First of all we ... On arrival I ... I observed ... Eventually, we ... And finally we ...". While she was writing she put her thinking into words so the children could get an idea of some of the thought processes needed when writing, for example "I have to think about how I am going to start this account ... I want to use some different words to start my sentences ... I can't use the phrase 'and then' too often or my writing won't be very interesting ... How shall I finish this account? I know, I'll use the phrase 'and finally we'".

## A trip to Castle Rising – session one

The educator's aim for this writing work was for the children to complete an account of their visit to the castle. She knew that the children would probably be good at sequencing the things that happened, but she wanted them to include some description and even some examples of things people said while on the visit.

A storyboard was used in the first session as a way to help the children organise the structure. The educator encouraged them to include people in their drawings with speech bubbles for what the people were saying. The educator explained that their accounts would be made into a class display for people to read, including the class, their own parents and other children in school. The children were excited to hear that there was an audience for their writing.

## A trip to Castle Rising – session two

This session began with a reminder of the work done the previous day, but the educator was keen to get the children writing quickly. The educator explained that the children were to turn their storyboard into a piece of writing. She discussed with the children what their challenges for their writing could be. Together they agreed to do at least three things: a) remember enough of the key events of the day in the right order; b) include some description; c) include at least one example of people talking.

The children who required extra support for their writing worked with the educator to put laminated versions of the photos in the appropriate sequence. More of this kind of oral work was done so that the children would have more confidence to do their writing. One word for one photo was appropriate for a minority of children in this group; others were encouraged to write one sentence for each photo.

As this session progressed some children completed a first draft. The educator provided each child with oral and written feedback and the children were able to mark any edits in a different coloured pen before writing out their second draft. Children ready to write the second draft were given the option of doing this on one of three class computers. This option further motivated children to persist with their writing and refocussed them on the audience for their writing. The children who had completed a second draft of their writing, which they were satisfied with themselves, either on the computer or hand written, shared their writing with a friend. They were able to make suggestions to each other. When the children and educator were happy with their second draft, the children knew they could engage in additional activities such as working in the writing area, using construction materials to build castles to inspire future story writing, or creating imaginative stories in the role play area.

## A trip to Castle Rising – session three

Part of the writing process comprises editing and proofreading. This is more meaningful if the writing is to be displayed or 'published' in some way. On this occasion the educator had decided to make a display. The wall display included a piece of writing from each child. The surface

### Aims for writing sessions with six year olds

**Teaching aims**

- Children write an account of an educational visit, inspired by their own interests and a shared real life experience.

- Children write for the audience who will see the class display.

- Children develop their editing, computer and presentation skills.

- Children decide what they need to improve in their writing to make it clear for an audience.

- Children learn how to write a good introductory paragraph with confidence.

**Assessment evidence in children's language**

- "I can write a report about a trip."

- "I can type my report up and see it on the display."

- "I can remember what happened when we went to Castle Rising."

- "I learned some new words and this made my writing more interesting."

- "I can show my mum my work and tell her what I did."

display included models of castles that the children had made from a variety of construction materials.

## Ending the writing sessions

The same plenary after each session can be boring for children so the educator had developed a range of quick and meaningful session conclusions. One of the most productive was when she used examples of the children's

writing on the visualiser to talk about the things that the class liked and how the writing could be developed. Other examples included:

- The children practising reading their writing so that they could read their writing aloud to the class confidently

- The children using the display to show their writing to other children and to their parents at the beginning of the school day.

The following example shows how one child experienced the sessions and what the outcomes were for her writing.

## Mini case study: Khadijah's writing

Khadijah was five years and four months old. The teaching assistant recorded her contributions to class discussions.

Recalling their visit to Castle Rising Khadijah said, "We went to Castle Rising on the bus! When we got there we went inside. We saw some ropes and we had to climb some steps. We saw a deep well in the ground. Then we went outside to eat our sandwiches. I had cucumber sandwiches. Then we played galloping. It was a long way home".

The session continued with Khadijah's storyboard version (see Figure 3.4).

Khadijah wrote out her first draft (see Figure 3.5) and then chose to complete the second draft (Figure 3.6) on the computer. This draft was put on the class wall display.

The educator was clear that she wanted the children to develop their writing based on an interest they had demonstrated themselves and then to extend it through a shared real life experience, the educational visit to Castle Rising. It has been common for sessions to be dominated by the educator's lesson objectives and for children to have to write these in their exercise books. If this is done repeatedly, it is not particularly interesting for the children. It should be regarded as a teaching strategy to be used occasionally as a way to focus a particular kind of session.

# HIGH QUALITY LITERACY TEACHING

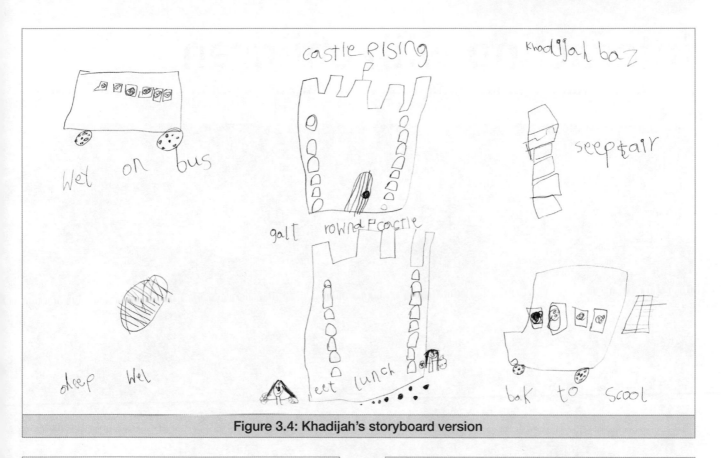

**Figure 3.4: Khadijah's storyboard version**

**Figure 3.5: Khadijah's first draft**

We went to Castle Rising on the bus. We went up lots ov seep sairs. We sor a worter wel it wos a long wai down. We galt rownd the castle on pretend hors. I had a cookumber sandwich. It wos rainng. We went bak to scool.

Khadijah Baz

**Figure 3.6: Khadijah's second draft**

# Interacting with children

**Interacting in small informal groups allows everyone to join in**

One of the most important features of educators' practice is the way that they interact with children. This interaction happens in three main contexts: a) talking to the whole class; b) talking to children in small groups; c) talking to individual children. Most research on interaction has looked at educators working with groups of children. One thing that educators need to be mindful about is the tendency to dominate interaction during group interaction: a balance of two thirds educator talk to one third pupil talk has been found in research[1]. When the one third of pupil talk is divided by 30 children in a class, this means that pupils are in danger of saying very little during whole class discussion. One important way to increase pupil talk time in this context is to encourage talk partners, pairs

of children who are encouraged to have brief conversations about points relevant to the teaching. The opportunity to sing songs together or to join in for sections of books and poems also increases the percentage, although this kind of chanting fulfils a more limited but important function.

One pattern of educator–pupil interaction that has been commonly observed is the initiation, response, feedback (IRF) pattern[2]. The initiation by the educator begins the fragment of interaction, the response comes from a pupil, then the educator confirms or corrects the response. While this form of interaction serves a particular purpose, and it could be argued to a certain extent arises naturally from

---

1   Flanders N A (1970) *Analysing Teacher Behaviour*. Addison-Wesley, Reading MA, USA.

2   Hardman F, Abd-Kadir J (2010). Classroom discourse: Towards a dialogic pedagogy. In D Wyse, R Andrews, J Hoffman (eds) *The Routledge International Handbook of English, Language and Literacy Teaching*. Routledge, London, UK.

# INTERACTING WITH CHILDREN

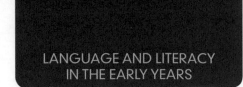

the socio-cultural context of classrooms, it is too limited on its own. In particular it is important that educators look for opportunities to make pupils active participants in the dialogue and to encourage children to articulate their ideas as much as possible. The use of open questions such as "so what did you like about that story?" and "why did the girl jump?" is one example of how to help with this. Another way is to resist the urge to offer feedback in order to concentrate on extending the dialogue.

Much of this research has been done with primary and secondary age children rather than with the youngest children. In early years settings, songs, rhymes and games are a form of interaction structure that, in addition to their intrinsic value, serve as a means to maintain young children's attention productively. The reading of stories to groups of children offers many opportunities for a variety of forms of interaction. However, a great deal of interaction takes place when children are playing. In these situations it is important for educators to try as much as possible to talk to the children as equals. Joining in with children's play can be a good strategy for engaging them in dialogue. But, as is the case with children and pupils of any age, the appropriate mutually trusting relationships have to be built as a foundation for productive dialogue.

Adults support children's talk by:

- Providing places for talk where children feel safe and secure. Children respond to different places but do talk the most where they like to play the most

- Listening to what the children are saying, scribing their words and reflecting on what has been said

- Listening to children talking in pairs and small groups as they are engaged in their play

- Acknowledging that children need support to learn to talk confidently to each other and to learn from each other

- Asking questions that keep the flow of dialogue, questions that are genuine rather than artificial

- Providing resources and opportunities that encourage and support children to speak freely and with growing confidence

- Providing a video camera with a built in microphone can inspire the most reluctant to vocalise, experiment with the different vocal sounds they can make and to sing songs

- Presenting children with photographs of real life experiences they have all shared

- Re-proposing children's talk, even a day or two later, helps them to build on what they have said before.

## Two children interacting with an adult

In Figure 4.1 two children interact with an adult in the workshop or modelling area of provision. The two boys, aged four years old, are working in parallel using cardboard boxes and masking tape to construct their rockets.

The skill of the adult is in listening to the children and only speaking occasionally. In this way the children's conversation is allowed to flow without adult interruption.

**Gaining confidence in speaking**

Figure 4.1 shows the adult's initiation and the child's response. Sometimes feedback comes from another child.

Adults model quality talk for children by:

- Playing alongside children and describing what they are doing

- Using the correct language for all the resources being used

- Maintaining eye contact and smiling to reassure

- In the way educators communicate with each other

- Listening carefully to the children's responses when they speak and repeating them so that the children hear the correct word order, grammar and vocabulary in a way that does not discourage.

If adults engage in play alongside children, listen to what they say, support them with respect, and manage the flow of talk, children will increasingly use narrative in their talk as they play.

When educators are tuned in to children's voices and enrich children's contributions in this way and children have access to developing their narratives within their self-initiated play, educators are able to introduce talk about literacy in a natural and non-threatening way. It is a part of the dialogue between children and adults and between children.

**Playing and interacting with a child engaged in water play**

## Joe's language and literacy

The following series of post-it observations, made by the educator, illustrates Joe's developing awareness of literacy.

5th November 2010: Joe looks at the book *The Three Little Pigs*. He shows me that he can point at the words. He attempts to read from left to right pointing at the text and tells the story as he knows it. He says, "I'll huff and puff with my chinny chin chin".

8th November 2010: Joe stands at the letter chart and he correctly says the sounds for 's', 'a', 't', 'p', 'i', 'n', 'm', 'd', 'g', 'o', 'c'. Joe chooses to read some tricky words: I, no, go, to, the.

12th November 2010: Joe is sitting beside me just before lunchtime. We are looking at a book about dinosaurs. Joe points to the pictures and the writing appropriately. He comments on a picture of a pterodactyl. Joe says, "He's sad because his wings are going to get wet". He is intrigued by the detail of the illustrations.

16th November 2010: Joe enjoys our phonics session with three of his friends. He is confident in blending when playing the I Spy game. Well done Joe!

# INTERACTING WITH CHILDREN

## Figure 4.1: Dialogue between two children and one adult in the modelling area

| Description | Commentary |
|---|---|
| **Rehan:** I want to make a rocket ... *(He selects a box)* These are the boosters for the rocket. That's the fire. | Rehan directs his talk to the adult. He is using talk successfully to describe his intentions. |
| **Karolis:** I'm making a real rocket. | Karolis considers his rocket to be better than Rehan's. |
| **Rehan:** Blast off! | |
| **Karolis:** You can see I've got fire. Those are my scissors. | While describing his rocket Karolis makes sure he doesn't lose his scissors. |
| **Rehan:** Don't fall down! This is a rocket. Rockets are good. | Rehan directs his speech to his model and then switches to the adult. |
| **Adult:** Why are they good? | The adult initiates by asking a genuine question: she really wants to know what Rehan means. |
| **Rehan:** Because they fly to the moon. | Rehan responds. |
| **Adult:** To the moon, that's amazing. | The adult provides feedback |
| **Karolis:** 'Cos you need to cut those off. On here and on here and on here. | Karolis is keen to share his model-making skills. His talk emphasises what you need to do. |
| **Rehan:** These are for the rocket. These are the windows. | Rehan continues with his explanation. |
| **Karolis:** But he's not got fire. See here, I'm going to put real fire. *Karolis points to the place on his model.* | |
| **Rehan:** I am fixing the windows with tape. The rocket fall down. | |
| **Karolis:** There's going to be two fires! | |
| **Rehan:** I need bottles. | |
| **Karolis:** Here how you make a window. | The two children describe what they are doing. Karolis likes to direct Rehan. |
| **Rehan:** This is how you make a window. | |
| **Karolis:** Blast off! *Karolis checks that the window is fastened securely.* | |
| **Karolis:** Teacher he not making a rocket, it got to be like this. | Karolis believes he knows how to make a model rocket and he wants Rehan to follow him. Rehan counteracts Karolis by re-labelling his model and calling it a "car rocket". |
| **Rehan:** It's a car rocket! | |
| **Karolis:** I've found something. | |
| *Karolis has found a long piece of corrugated paper. The adult explains what it is and introduces the word 'corrugated'. The two children have a go saying it themselves.* | Here the adult has intervened to provide the children with information they do not already know. |
| **Rehan:** I'm tricking you, it's a rocket. | This dialogue emphasises children's ability to return to themes. In this section Rehan decides his model is a rocket and Karolis is now happy for him to label it so. The adult initiates a response. Karolis responds, by saying he is teasing. The adult feeds back and asks for confirmation which Rehan does with a touch of humour. |
| **Adult:** But I thought you said it's a car rocket. | |
| **Karolis:** He's teasing you, it's a rocket. | |
| **Adult:** So just a rocket, it doesn't turn into a car? | |
| **Rehan:** No, it was a tease! I'm going to show my uncle. I can make anything. | |
| *The adult remarks that the area of provision has been labelled "workshop".* | Once again the adult initiates a development in the conversation and encourages the children to be aware of environmental print. Rehan responds and shows that he understands what children are expected to do in this area and has possibly come up with a better name. |
| **Rehan:** No, "making shop". | |
| *Rehan has cut up pieces of corrugated paper and put them inside the bottle he has attached to his model.* | |

Figure 4.1: Dialogue between two children and one adult in the modelling area (continued)

| Description | Commentary |
|---|---|
| **Rehan:** Look what I've put in the bottle. I'm trying to get it out. It makes a noise.<br><br>*Rehan comments on hearing a child speak in another language.* | As the session proceeds the children continue to describe the process of making their rockets. |
| **Rehan:** Another language. It's not English.<br>**Adult:** What's the other language you can speak?<br>**Karolis:** I can do that other language. A – B – C!<br>*Karolis says "ABC" using a deep voice.*<br>**Rehan:** A monster language!<br>*Everyone laughs.*<br>*The adult continues to observe the two children as they construct their model rockets.*<br>*The adult notices that Karolis has cut a green circle into quarters.*<br>**Adult to Karolis:** I like the way you have cut the circle into quarters. | Rehan and Karolis are both bilingual as are most children in the setting. Rehan listens and comments. This prompts the adult to ask about the languages they speak. Karolis's response is both unexpected and valid. Humour signifies a shared understanding. |
| **Karolis:** I did this. Cut! Cut! Cut! And then I did like this.<br>*A third child has joined the workshop area. He takes one of the strips of masking tape Karolis has cut off ready.*<br>**Karolis:** He is all the time taking big.<br>**Adult:** You don't always need long pieces of tape.<br><br>**Rehan:** This is a rocket. You have to cut these, that's how you make a rocket.<br>*The three children continue to construct their models. When it is time to tidy away Rehan and Karolis put their models on the side to return to later.* | Karolis likes to repeat what he says three times, for emphasis. This is a recurring theme.<br><br><br>The adult recasts by confirming what Karolis has said using standard English and doesn't impede the flow of talk.<br>Rehan uses talk to restate and reaffirm. |

## Next steps

- Develop Karolis' and Rehan's knowledge and understanding of rockets and space by taking them to the school library to find books and to look for information on the internet.

- Teach design and technology skills to improve their ability to join and fix.

- Show Karolis and Rehan that they can use their models in the small world and construction areas.

- Scribe the narratives that arise from their small world play.

- Take photographs of this process and create a learning story.

- Encourage their parents to take them to a space museum, located close to the setting.

CHAPTER 5

# Multilingualism

**Sharing a story in the child's home language**

A notable report from the 1970s argued that "every teacher is a teacher of language"[1]. Since that time educators, researchers and policy makers have tried to match the rhetoric of this admirable assertion with a more coherent understanding of how this might work in practice. An important starting point is the educator's perspectives on language. In nearly every educational setting children arrive with a very wide range of language experiences. Although multiple language use is particularly varied in cities, due to migration patterns, in nearly every class in rural areas there will be children who can speak more than one language. Even a quick glance at the national curricula of Scotland and Wales reveals fully equal Welsh bilingualism and two strands of Gaelic in Scotland. Multilingualism is the norm.

There is strong research evidence to show that support for home languages that children bring to the setting is likely to result in better outcomes, not only for those languages but for the learning of English as well[2]. This does not mean that educators need to be able to speak the other languages that children use (although this, and the use of bilingual teaching assistants, is of course invaluable). Rather it is necessary for educators to be positive about the language abilities that children bring to the setting. One simple but powerful way to demonstrate this positive attitude and to enhance all the children's learning is to carry out a language survey of the class. These surveys seek to answer questions such as: "Which languages do you speak?" "Which languages

1   Department of Education and Science (1975) *A Language for Life* [the Bullock report]. Her Majesty's Stationery Office, London, UK.

2   Reese L, Garnier H, Gallimore R, Goldenberg C (2000) Longitudinal analysis of the antecedents of emergent Spanish literacy and middle-school English reading achievement of Spanish-speaking students. *American Educational Research Journal*, 37(3), 622-633.

do you use in different settings such as home, school and religious settings?" "Which languages do your family speak?" Another straightforward demonstration of a positive attitude to multilingualism is to have posters that feature words in different languages, particularly those languages that are most relevant to the class. Educators should also learn a few phrases and help children to learn them too. The resources of the classroom can also represent the children's languages, for example the use of dual language texts as part of the resources for reading.

Periodically, migration results in new waves of families coming from other countries to work in the UK. In recent years workers from eastern Europe have come to the UK, and this has presented opportunities and challenges for educators. There are special circumstances for children who speak no English when they join the setting. Settings should have in place a process for helping these children. This will include recognition that most children new to a language need to spend a lot of time listening at first. Simple communication used daily, such as greetings, will help these children make their first steps into learning the new language.

Because language is so important to all teaching, educators need to be guided by appropriate linguistic principles[3]:

- Communication of understandable meaning is the driving force of language

- Analysis of language in use is the basis for appropriate knowledge for pupils and educators

- As a consequence of the natural processes of language change, descriptive accounts of language are more appropriate than prescriptive accounts

- Experiencing and reflecting on the processes of reading and writing are an important resource to enhance teaching and learning

- Language and social status (or power) are inextricably linked.

## Support for multilingual children

As is the case for all children in the setting, a home visit needs to be planned (see Chapter 1) when it is known that a family new to the country is joining the setting. It can be a challenge for a family new to the country to understand the nature of home visits. The availability of another more established member of the community during the home visit can be a great help with communication. If this is not possible, then visual support such as photographs from the setting can be helpful.

The educators' knowledge of the children's home experience informs their provision for the home area of the setting. Purchasing additional domestic utensils from the local shops that are particularly relevant to new children's home experience will mean they immediately see something familiar. In general, the continuous provision that is of benefit to all children will also benefit children new to English, because it gives them easy access to physical resources that are a good starting point for language and learning.

Visual references are a vital area of support, for example photographs illustrating the sequence of daily events in the setting. Special events can also be shown. These photos can also be an aid to discussions with the child's parents.

The identification of child buddies who speak the same language as the child is invaluable in the early years setting. If the setting is located within a primary school site, it could be possible to find an older buddy who will have the maturity to explain what is happening in the setting in the child's first language. If the child who is new to the setting becomes upset, 'sending' for the buddy provides great reassurance and can avoid the need to contact the child's parent or carer.

Some settings learn how to improve their practice by asking the parents or carers, some time later, to reflect on the induction experience. Consultation with parents and carers is a helpful way to find out where practice can be embedded and improved.

Record-keeping in the setting needs to include a clear focus on communication, particularly for multilingual children. The

3   Wyse D (2011) The control of language or the language of control? Primary teachers' knowledge in the context of policy. In S Ellis, E McCarthy (eds) *Applied Linguistics and the Primary School.* Cambridge University Press, Cambridge, UK.

# MULTILINGUALISM

educator needs to be especially alert as to whether the child is using non-verbal communication effectively so that their immediate needs are being met. Some educators not only support the child through exaggerated actions that illustrate forms of communication, but also teach signing to support communication between the child and adult as well as between the child and other children.

Multilingual educators are able to scribe the child's talk in their first language. This information can be used to inform the assessment process. The following observation illustrates the process of scribing a child's talk in Mirpuri Punjabi, then reflecting on the child's development and identifying next steps for the educator to extend the child's learning. (Mirpuri Punjabi does not have a written script so the educator has scribed the child's talk phonetically.)

## Child observation showing how a multilingual educator scribed the child's talk

Farkarn is four years old and he has just started attending school. His first language is Mirpuri Punjabi. Farkarn decides to go to the home area and play in the kitchen. He puts a cooking pot on the gas and uses a spoon to stir with.

Adult: Thusa kyah karaney hoo?
*What are you doing?*

Farkarn: Kanna paka raha ho!
*I'm making the food!*

Adult: Kis k liya?
*Who for?*

Farkarn: Arp k liya.
*For you.*

Adult: Kya bana raha ho?
*What are you cooking?*

Farkarn: Pakora buna raha ho!
*I am cooking pakora!*

Adult: Kitne dehr lagah gee? Mujha bhook lagee hai.
*How long will it take? I'm hungry.*

Farkarn: Thuk na ina karma table the ha va nah.
*Look, there's so much food on the table already.*

Adult: Pakora no kinee dheer lagah gee?
*How long will the pakora take?*

Farkarn: Booht dheer.
*Too long.*

Farkarn: Thuk bun geeya.
*Look they're cooked.*

Farkarn shows confidence in speaking and listening in Mirpuri Punjabi. He is receptive to the educator's questions and he readily involves her in his play. His conversation relates to his home experience. Farkarn uses talk to answer questions, describe his actions and to engage in imaginative play. This observation shows the value of home area provision that reflects the child's own home.

Next steps:

- To further enrich Farkarn's learning in school, prepare some real food with Farkarn, letting him decide what to prepare

- Support Farkarn in writing a shopping list and take a small group of children shopping for the food

- Take photographs of this experience and create a learning story to share with his friends in school and his parents

- Invite Farkarn's parents to contribute to his learning story.

## Planning for multilingual learners

Planning for multilingual learners includes support for their understanding of what is expected in the setting. Talk partners are an effective way of providing children with the time to articulate their understanding about what they are doing and learning. Multilingual learners benefit from having time to talk in English and other languages.

Multilingual learners benefit from having visual prompts to support their understanding. The best visual prompts are real objects. The educator needs to spend some additional time making collections of objects to make meaning visible. For example, when leading a discussion about 'home' the educator needs to have the doll's house in the vicinity to ensure children understand the detail of the talk. Using the indoor and outdoor learning environments as a constant resource to reinforce vocabulary is an essential ingredient of the multilingual child's experience.

To introduce a new story to multilingual learners the educators can perform the story for the children. Not all children understand that stories can be performed and before they can be expected to take part in role play based on a story, they need to observe others. A team of educators took some Year 1 children to a small hall area to perform the story of *Goldilocks and the Three Bears*. This was the launch for their work based on this traditional tale. Immediately all the children were engaged and the performance became a meaningful reference point for everyone throughout the following three weeks.

Planning demonstrations is another proven strategy for supporting young multilingual learners. A demonstration is when an adult shows the children how to do something, for example how to mix dry powder paint, how to make pasta, how to sew, how to build a brick wall. Some demonstrations lead to the children learning the skill for themselves, others are for observation and discussion. Builders on site are an example of the latter, when children are given the opportunity to see people engaged in the world of work. However, there are other occasions where a visiting adult demonstrates a skill, for example paper-making, and it is possible to then provide the materials for the children to follow up the demonstration with the real experience.

However, this strategy only works for multilingual learners if the adult provides the commentary. For example a chef visiting one setting demonstrated how he prepared a fish for cooking. The educator supported the chef in providing a detailed commentary including precise vocabulary. The impact of this demonstration was that the children became fascinated by fish and wanted to find out more, so reference to non-fiction books became meaningful.

These strategies of talk partners, visual prompts, role playing stories and demonstrations are relevant to all children and are essential for children acquiring English.

## Dhobi Eyer! The Washerman Comes! Three year olds

In order to help all the children in the setting to learn about language, and to support children new to English, an educator decided to teach a song in Urdu. None of the children spoke Urdu but there was a local community nearby that did. The educators were keen for the children to learn the song to broaden not only the children's but also their families' awareness and perceptions. The setting explained the approach to the families, and as a result the work was positively supported by them.

The song is sung to the tune of Frère Jacques (extended). The lines "Dhobi eyer" and "Capray liar" are both sung to the tune of the first line of Frère Jacques.

| Urdu | English |
| --- | --- |
| Dhobi eyer | Washerman coming |
| Dhobi eyer | Washerman coming |
| Capray liar | Bringing clothes |
| Capray liar | Bringing clothes |
| Capray sarf | Clothes are clean |
| Capray sarf | Clothes are clean |
| Kitnay capray liar? | How many clothes? |
| Kitnay capray liar? | How many clothes? |
| Ayk doh teen | One two three |
| Char paanch chay | Four five six |
| Saat aht nor | Seven eight nine |
| Das or bus! | Ten and stop! |

## Dhobi Eyer! The Washerman Comes! Session one

During a 10 minute singing session the educator introduced the song by explaining she had learnt it from someone she had met on a course (the children become familiar with the idea that sometimes educators are not present because they are continuing to learn themselves). She then sang the song. The educator explained that the children at her friend's setting speak many different languages. The educator asked the children if they knew any other languages. One child explained that they went on holiday to Spain and he had learnt to say "Hola!"

Providing different scripts inspires
children to try writing them

Performing a new story is an effective way
of introducing it to multilingual children

## Dhobi Eyer! The Washerman Comes! Session two

The educator asked the children if they recalled the song she sang yesterday and what it was about. She used a puppet dressed as a washerman. As she sang the song she acted out the meaning using the puppet. Before singing the song a second time she suggested that the children join in with the last word, 'bus!', meaning 'stop!' The children joined in and the educator noted that some of the children were attempting the numbers. They sang the song for a third time, emphasising the numbers. She brought the singing session to an end. Some children continued to sing as they played.

## Dhobi Eyer! The Washerman Comes! Session three

On the third day, the educator, with another colleague, encouraged the children to join in with the actions and to sing along. She explained that when they went outside to play they could wash the dolls' clothes like the dhobi did. This meant getting them soapy and thrashing them on the ground. The children enjoyed this opportunity to bring the song to life.

## Dhobi Eyer! The Washerman Comes! Session four

To start the fourth session the educator showed the children the photographs of themselves washing the dolls' clothes outside. The children had also started singing the song outside and were now eager to participate in singing the song again. The educator showed the children images of washermen working in Pakistan and India. She suggested that they might like to illustrate the words of the songs in the writing area.

This follow-up activity encouraged the children to make the link between the spoken word and the written word. The children described their pictures and remembered the words 'dhobi' meaning washerman and 'capray' meaning clothes.

Figure 5.1: A dhobi illustration

Figure 5.2: Another dhobi illustration

## Dhobi Eyer! The Washerman Comes! Session five

In this last singing session of the week the educator showed the children the pictures some of the children had drawn. The children sang the complete song enthusiastically and were excited about taking the words and their own illustration (see Figures 5.1 and 5.2) home to share with their families. In the art area photocopies of their illustrations were available for them to add colour using either powder paint, or watercolours or coloured inks.

Within a language-rich environment, multilingual children will readily talk about their ability to speak different languages and the language skills of family members. It is the educator's role to tune into this talk about languages, to scribe what the children say and ask questions to find out more about their linguistic capabilities. In Figure 5.3, the visiting adult sits with a group of five- and six-year-old mono- and multilingual learners who are working on telling the time. Julia and Natasha are multilingual and Ellie speaks one language, English. They are all girls. Wilson is a boy.

### Aims for multilingual singing sessions with three year olds

**Teaching aims**

- Develop children's awareness of different languages.

- Develop children's ability to learn and sing a new song.

- Encourage children's curiosity about cultures other than their own.

- For children to learn about how the dhobi does the washing and how this relates to their own lives.

**Assessment evidence in children's language**

- "I know some Urdu words!"

- "I can sing all the words!"

# MULTILINGUALISM

## Figure 5.3: A group of children and an adult discuss language

| Description | Commentary |
| --- | --- |
| **Julia:** Why you come here?<br>**Ellie:** She's Polish.<br>**Julia:** What's your name?<br>**Adult:** Christine.<br>**Julia:** Lovely name. | Immediately Julia is asking the visiting adult questions showing personal confidence and confidence in her ability to speak English. Another child informs the adult that Julia is Polish. Does the second child recognise that Julia's question was grammatically incorrect? |
| **Natasha:** I can speak different languages. I can speak Italian, I can speak English, I can speak Polish ... | Natasha picks up on Ellie's prompt about languages and proceeds to inform the adult of her knowledge of languages. |
| *The children are asked to return to the carpet area. The children are told an extract from the Christmas story. The children are asked to work in their literacy groups and continue their nativity stories which they are writing and illustrating.* | |
| **Natasha continues:** ... and I can speak Portuguese ... This is how you really draw people. | Natasha shows continued need to inform the adult of her knowledge. |
| *Natasha describes how to draw a stick person.* | The adult picks up on Natasha's cue that languages are important. The adult wants to show Natasha that she values this information and knowledge. |
| *The adult asks Natasha why she knows so many languages.* | |
| **Natasha:** Our mummy speaks Portuguese, Italian, Polish and English. There's a school disco today and I'm going to wear what I wore to the Christening ... Our mum's crazy sometimes. *Natasha laughs.* | Natasha responds positively to the question. She moves from one subject to another. This is common amongst young children and needs to be recognised by educators as a developmental characteristic, not confusion. |
| *Natasha informs the adult that another child, Wilson, speaks Portuguese. The adult invites Wilson over to the table and he smiles. The adult, Natasha and Wilson talk about eating snails with lots of garlic.* | Natasha understands that the adult is interested in children's ability to speak different languages and invites another child into the conversation. |
| *Natasha returns to her writing.* | |
| **Natasha:** You always write 'and' in sentences. | Natasha shares her understanding of writing conventions. |
| *Natasha shows the adult the different types of exercise books they have.* | Natasha is now keen to inform the adult of other aspects of school life and in this instance she chooses their exercise books. The adult is interested in what she has to say and Natasha has recognised this. |
| **Natasha:** We have different types of books here. This is our one. | |
| *The book is labelled "topic".* | |
| **Natasha:** I think this is our spelling book. This is our number work book. | |
| *Natasha points to a child's name.* | |
| **Natasha:** Julia. This is our last one. | |
| **Adult:** What is it? | |
| **Natasha:** Literacy. Have you had any lunch yet? What's your school called? | Natasha turns her attention to the visiting adult's needs, such as has she eaten, and where she works. |
| *Adult responds.* | |
| **Natasha:** [Name of school] I think I've heard of it before. | |

### Next steps

- Focus on the number of different languages spoken in the class. Everyone learns basic words in every language.
- Collect one song in every language for the children to learn.
- Make the songs into a book for the children to illustrate.
- Provide plans of the school grounds for the children to annotate.
- Create different trails around school highlighting different features.

# Working with multilingual reading resources

There are many books available for young children written in more than one language. In addition to these texts, it is important to have books written in a single language other than English to reflect the languages spoken in the setting and community. In addition, listening equipment placed alongside the book area can be used to provide opportunities for children to hear both stories and songs in a range of languages.

With the provision of bilingual and multilingual books, educators can share these texts with either individual children or small groups of children. This allows for children to ask their own questions about the texts and the language.

Continuous provision of these texts is enhanced by the planning for a series of sessions to draw children's attention to the texts.

## Hello World![4] Session one

The educator introduces the five minute session by welcoming the children in a language other than English. He asks the children if they know any other ways of saying "Hello!" The educator then explains that he wants to go on holiday to Germany and maybe the book he has brought to share could help them to find out how to say "Good morning!" He reads fragments of the book until he finds "Guten Morgen". To finish the session he places the book on the book shelf in a prominent place and plans to note if any children choose to look at the book for themselves.

## Hello World! Session two

The educator has invited a parent to introduce the second session. As a result of the setting's newsletter a child's mother who is a fluent Italian speaker offered to speak to the children in her first language. The children are fascinated to hear one of the parents speak in another language. They are delighted to show her their book and where it says "Ciao!" The children are encouraged by the educator to ask the parent questions about being Italian: What food does she like? Does she listen to Italian songs? Can she sing an Italian nursery rhyme? How does *Twinkle Twinkle Little Star* go in Italian? The children find out that pizza and pasta are Italian. The educator invites the parent to return another time to demonstrate how she makes pasta.

## Hello World! Session three

The educator has noticed in his observations that the children are increasingly interested in the book. To begin the session the educator reads it all the way through, noting which greetings the children are most interested in. The educator suggests to the children that they can make their own greetings book. He has prepared some ready-made books by simply folding pieces of A4 card in half. He has also prepared different greetings in different languages on small strips of paper. He explains that when they go to

---

### Aims for reading sessions with three year olds

**Teaching aims**

- Develop children's awareness of different languages spoken in the community.

- Develop the children's enjoyment of listening to different languages.

- Learn to say greetings in different languages.

**Assessment evidence in children's language**

- "I know lots of languages!"

- "Listen to me! Bonjour!"

---

4   Stojic M (2009) *Hello World!* Boxer Books Limited, London, UK.

# MULTILINGUALISM

the mark-making area they can select a book and use the strips of paper to stick into their own book, choosing their favourite greetings. A copy of the book is available to the children so that they can decide the country of origin of each greeting. The educator asks the children how they might illustrate their own book. One child suggests that they draw a picture of someone they know who speaks that language. The educator asks them: "What do you do if you do not know someone?" The child responds: "Make someone up".

The children respond enthusiastically to the idea of creating their own books. They question each other about the languages they speak. They ask their educator if anyone else in the setting speaks another language. The educator responds by giving the children a list of all the adults working in the setting and the different languages they speak. As he reads it through to the children they decide to invite some of the adults to their room so that they can hear another language being spoken. The educator takes this unplanned opportunity to scribe the wording for the invitations with the children. They make suggestions about what they should say but at the same time the educator reinforces the conventions of writing an invitation. The task of preparing the invitations is offered to those children who are not making books.

## Working with multilingual writing resources

Young children are intrigued by different languages and different written scripts. Making a range of scripts visible motivates talk about similarities and differences between languages. Provision of different scripts in the writing area creates opportunities for children to have a go at writing them. Children respond positively to seeing greetings cards, menus, newspapers and magazines in different scripts and these can be included as part of the continuous provision. It is effective to plan a focus on a particular script to link with celebrations throughout the year. For example, young children enjoy writing words in Chinese when focussing on Chinese New Year celebrations; the Arabic script can

be a focus during the observance of Eid. Having different types of mark-makers also promotes the visibility of different scripts, for example Chinese pens for Chinese writing and using bamboo pens in a clay slip (clay mixed with water to produce the consistency of ready-mixed paint) for writing the Arabic alphabet. Children will make their own version of the scripts through their mark-making. For the youngest children, the expectation is not for every child to participate in these activities, but that they have access to them within the continuous provision and are aware of the possibilities. Children in Key Stage 1 are ready to present different scripts with more accuracy.

The focus on modern foreign languages in Key Stage 2 can have a positive impact on the younger children's perceptions of different languages. Knowledge of different languages can be shared by older children with younger children, through classroom visits, presentations in assembly and articles in school newsletters and on the school website. Educators are confident to share their knowledge when the ethos of the school promotes and celebrates a range of languages. Nursery age children will happily respond to greetings in different languages. The educator's personal experiences of travel can enhance the children's awareness of the wider world. Christine explained to her class of three and four year olds that she was travelling to Italy[5]. She showed the children her Italian dictionary and asked them for suggestions about the words she needed on her travels. The children were able to offer their suggestions which included "Where is the toilet?" or "Dove gabinetto?"

On her return to the nursery, Christine brought her experience of visiting Italy back to the setting and different lines of inquiry were explored, including writing postcards, talking about children in another country and the similarities and differences between their lives there and in the UK and drawing maps of the journey to Italy.

The principal role for the educator is to be receptive to the opportunities for talk and extending the children's knowledge and understanding as they arise. If a learning opportunity arises through real events and experiences the impact will be more profound for each individual child.

5   Parker C (2001) "She's back!" The impact of my visit to Reggio Emilia on a group of 3- and 4-year-olds. In L Abbott, C Nutbrown (eds) *Experiencing Reggio Emilia: Implications for pre-school provision*. Open University Press, Buckingham, UK.

# Assessing language and literacy

**An educator supports reading development**

As we argued in Chapter 1, educators need to build on what children know in order to help them learn most effectively. But how do you know what children's prior understanding is? This is where assessment is such an important feature of educators' work. Assessment is frequently categorised as three main types: formative, summative and diagnostic[1]. When educators assess children relatively informally as part of day to day work in the setting, this is known as formative assessment. However, as with most category sets there can be overlaps. If, for example, the educator keeps records of their formative assessments over time then makes a judgement in relation to pre-determined criteria such as an early years profile, then the formative becomes summative. Similarly if the educator identifies a particular problem that a child is experiencing which leads to the discovery that the child needs some kind of special support, then this might be described as diagnostic assessment. However, our view is that there is already too much formal summative assessment built into national systems of education. It is formative assessment that is one of the most important facets of educators' professional skills. Effective formative

---

1    Johnson S (2011) *Assessing Learning in the Primary Classroom*. Routledge, London, UK.

# ASSESSING LANGUAGE AND LITERACY

assessment begins with the ability to observe with perception and sensitivity. With experience, and through reading of accounts of children's development, this perceptive observation is combined with knowledge of typical patterns of development.

Of the three modes of talking, reading and writing, talking is the most complex to assess. One of the reasons for this is that by the time children are five they will have acquired the majority of the linguistic attributes of talking for communication[2]. However, educators can support children's development of language in the earliest stages by enjoying varied opportunities to talk to children in a spirit of genuine interest and respect. One of the most important things to bear in mind when thinking about assessing talk is the way that the context will affect children's 'performance'. For example, seeing children interacting with the parents at home as opposed to in the setting will provide different contexts. Playing outside; playing in different areas inside; talking to close friends or talking to children who are less familiar are all contextual factors that will affect the nature of children's talk. Another major area is, of course, the languages that are spoken. Educators need as much information as possible about the languages and dialects that children use if they are to help them most effectively (see Chapter 5).

The mode of reading is perhaps the most assessed aspect of the curriculum as a whole. Perhaps the simplest and most powerful way to assess a child's reading is to share a book with them, discuss the book and keep informal records in a diary of observations. These observations can then inform future teaching as patterns emerge that are common areas of learning for different groups of children. One of the most important reasons for assessment of reading is to identify children who may struggle with reading. These children should be identified by the age of six at the latest and given extra support so that they do not fall behind[3]. However, this reading assessment should not be restricted to phonics only (nor should this become a dominant component in reading teaching[4]). It should account for the child's reading in general including reading comprehension, and their reading interests.

As far as writing is concerned one of the most important distinctions that should be made when assessing writing is between process and product. A piece of writing or mark-making on its own does reveal important aspects of children's writing development. But the assessment is so much more meaningful when examples or portfolios of writing are accompanied by notes about the processes that children go through when carrying out the writing.

Most settings collate each child's observations and organise them into a record book, often referred to as a Record of Achievement. In some settings these are organised chronologically then analysed in relation to government-designated areas of learning in the early years curriculum. Other settings organise the child observations according to which area of learning is most strongly evident from the child's learning at any particular time. The Record of Achievement needs to be child and parent/carer friendly, and families need to know that they can make a valuable contribution to their child's learning journey. Photographs, if permission has been given, further enhance a child's Record of Achievement as well as samples of their mark-making, writing and drawing. By the time a child has attended a setting for one year a wonderful picture of their development and learning is available to all. Children love to see the progress they have made themselves and to share that with educators and family members.

## Assessing talk

Scribing what children actually say, or recording some interaction then reflecting on it afterwards, is the best way to capture evidence for formative assessment of their talk. The examples of talk do not need to be very long but need to be selected carefully so that they are relevant to the focus of the assessment. Selecting what appear to be interesting moments in children's development is essential. It is important that any records of talk (or of any kind for that matter) are not so numerous that there is not time to analyse them and use the analysis to inform teaching. This is a real case of less is more!

2   Peccei J S (2006) *Child Language: A resource book for students*. Routledge, London, UK.

3   Clay M (1979) *The Early Detection of Reading Difficulties*. Third Edition. Heinemann Education, Auckland, New Zealand.

4   National Institute of Child Health and Human Development (2000) *National Reading Panel. Teaching children to read: An evidence-based assessment of the scientific research literature on reading and its implications for reading instruction. Reports of the subgroups* (NIH pub no. 00-4754). US Government Printing Office, Washington DC, USA.

Figures 6.1 to 6.4 show examples of transcriptions of children's talk.

Involving parents in their children's learning creates opportunities for parents to share their own observations of their child at home. Rosie is four years old and her mother has scribed her talk at home to share with educators at the setting (Figure 6.1).

In Figure 6.2, a five-year-old child is playing with sea life small world play. This observation was within a five minute time frame. It is rich with possibilities for developing Shannon's literacy learning within a context she understands and has ownership of.

In Figure 6.3, Kevins, Martin, Charlie, Adam, Daniel and Farid are all five years old and are involved in playing at the building site outside.

In Figure 6.4, Kirsty, Jack and Rory are five years old and are engaged in surgery role play. This observation is over a period of 20 minutes.

## Assessing children's literacy learning

### Learning stories

To deepen knowledge and understanding of each child, the implementation of 'learning stories'[5] enables early years educators to accompany an observation with a series of photographs. Each photograph is annotated to tell the story of the children's development and learning. Each child may have just one learning story in their Record of Achievement. The depth of understanding acquired through this process means that one story enriches the child's future literacy learning.

Figures 6.5 and 6.6 show examples of learning stories. Figure 6.5 illustrates what happened when Rehan, who attends a Foundation Stage/Reception class, wanted to have a turn on the interactive whiteboard.

Figure 6.6 illustrates the value of learning stories when early years educators document children's language and literacy learning in Year 2. The children are aged six and seven and in England educators have to submit national assessment data. It is important that a test-orientated curriculum is not seen as the main method of assessment for the children. Observations and work samples are the key processes to inform the summative educator assessments required. The theme of this learning story is Pamela's learning following a school visit from a nurse.

### Writing assessment

For all children in early years settings, writing assessment is not confined to what an educator has asked a child to do at a particular moment in time. Knowing about every child's writing is an on-going process. There are times when children demonstrate what they do best during self-selected activity.

Figures 6.7 to 6.12 show examples of children's writing at different ages alongside analysis of the processes, developmental aspects and the relevance that the examples had for the individual children concerned.

More samples of children's writing accompanied with a description of the context are to be found in Chapter 13.

### Reading assessment

Figure 6.13 shows an example of a reading assessment. Flo is in the Foundation class and is five years old. The educator, Ms Patel, has read the book, *Look at the Pencil*[6], with Flo and another child, Poppy. The educator has modelled one-to-one correspondence, using known words, initial sounds and pictures to read unfamiliar words. Flo then reads the book. Before reading a page she talks about what is happening in the picture. She is able to blend many words using her phonic knowledge. When she cannot read a word she looks at the pictures to help her make sense of the text. This is a running record of Flo re-reading the book. The ticks indicate when the word has been read correctly.

5   Carr M (2001) *Assessment in Early Childhood Settings: Learning stories*. Paul Chapman Publishing, London, UK.

6   Randell B, Giles J, Smith A (1999) *Look at the Pencil*. Nelson Cengage Learning, Victoria, Australia.

# ASSESSING LANGUAGE AND LITERACY

## Figure 6.1: A child's dialogue with her mother

| Transcription of a child's talk | Commentary |
|---|---|
| Rosie is drawing a picture of her family. | |
| Mum, I'm playing hobblesticks on this picture. I've got bare toes because everyone has to have bare toes to play fiddle balance. Shall I do it sunny day or a rainy day? | Rosie uses talk to describe, imagine and explain her picture. Rosie asks her mother for her opinion as she draws. |
| I'm writing names. Now I've got to do dots. Dotty is its name. I'm going to do a floating 'A' for Alice. Actually that would spoil the picture. I'm doing my family. | |
| One toe sticking out of that leg, two toes sticking out of that trouser leg. Mum, what else would you like? | Rosie shows that she has a rich vocabulary that she uses to great effect to describe her actions and her picture. |

## Figure 6.2: A child describes her small world play

| Transcription of a child's talk | Commentary |
|---|---|
| **Shannon:** Then he went on a boat. Then he fell back in the water. Then he found another boat. It was good enough for the other one. The boat kept sanking and in that boat making the sand wet in there. | Shannon uses talk to imagine and tell her story. |
| Then a crocodile came. | |
| Then a crocodile came. | Shannon builds up the drama of her story through repeated phrases. This is a construct she will have heard in stories and songs. |
| Then a crocodile came. | |
| A crocodile coming! | |
| *Shannon says "crocodile" in a high pitched voice.* | Shannon has learnt that you can change the pitch of your voice to dramatic effect. |
| **Shannon:** He snapped the boat! ... He got him! | |
| The crocodile has caught the man. | |
| Look here's a baby one ... I put them on a boat and they never be nasty to him anymore. Snapping each other. The crocodile snapped his tail and he bited his tail. | Shannon reaches a resolution and then decides to return to the fighting theme. |
| *Another child joins Shannon.* | |
| **Shannon:** Let me show you this. | Shannon is keen to share her story with another child. |

### Next steps

- Recast Shannon's talk so that she hears grammatically correct verbs in the past tense.
- Scribe one of Shannon's narratives, type it up and print it off.
- Show Shannon the script and record her response.
- Suggest to Shannon that she could illustrate her story. Alternatively take photographs of her story using the small world play resources. These can be shared with the whole class on either the interactive whiteboard or visualiser or in a display book.

## Figure 6.3: A group of children learn to play together on the building site role play area

| Transcription of a child's talk | Commentary |
|---|---|
| **Martin:** What do we do first? | Martin uses talk to get the group organised. Charlie takes a leadership role: he knows what they need to do and he understands where to find resources. |
| **Charlie:** We need some water. You have to get some from the tap. | |
| *Kevins tips the bucket of sand.* | |
| **Charlie:** Someone needs to help me 'cause it's heavy. | Charlie uses talk to reason. |
| *Adam comes to help out.* | |
| **Charlie:** We need the wheelbarrow. | Again, Charlie is directing his friends. |
| *Adam fills the wheelbarrow. He pushes the wheelbarrow and then tips the bricks out.* | |
| **Adam:** We've got lots now. | Adam uses talk to report. |
| **Daniel:** Shall we put it on here, on top? | Daniel uses questioning to find out others' opinions. |
| **Kevins:** Where? Where? Okay. We need to make it strong. We need to build it like this. | Kevins joins in with the questioning and then adds direction to the task by demonstrating what they need to do next, i.e. mixing the sand and water. |
| *Kevins points to the brickwork on the school wall and starts putting the sand and water mix in between.* | |
| **Farid:** We need to build it like this. Nice and high. | Farid joins in, giving his opinion on what they need to do. |
| *Farid holds his arm up to indicate the height.* | |
| **Kevins:** We can't. We don't have enough bricks. | Kevins intervenes with a problem: insufficient bricks. Charlie brings his solution: they need to downsize their project. |
| **Charlie:** We need to do it just a little bit. | |
| *All the children get to work using the trowels to spread the sand and water mix onto the bricks.* | |
| **Farid:** We dig, dig, dig all day. *(In a singing voice)* | The children are getting involved in the task and start singing their own digging song. |
| **Martin:** All morning and all night. *(In a singing voice)* | |
| *They make up words for the song.* | |
| *Charlie finds the spirit level.* | Charlie shows his curiosity when he finds the spirit level and asks the adult observer what it is. Following the explanation he starts to use it appropriately. |
| **Charlie:** What's this? *(Directed to the observer)* | |
| *Charlie listens to the adult's explanation and then uses the spirit level to check the level of the wall they are building.* | |

### Next steps

- Provide more time for children to play in the building site. Encourage other children to play alongside and with this group of children who can be role models for others. Particularly encourage girls to participate.

- Scribe the children's talk to re-present to them and highlight how much learning there is.

- Provide laminated building plans to enrich the play.

- Visit to see builders at work.

- Enhance the indoor construction area with non-fiction books about building.

# ASSESSING LANGUAGE AND LITERACY ....................

Figure 6.4: A group of children engaged in surgery role play

| Transcription of a child's talk | Commentary |
| --- | --- |
| *Kirsty goes to the role play area which is set up as a doctor's surgery. Then she revisits the writing area to collect a clipboard and a piece of paper. Kirsty returns to the surgery and writes on the clipboard. She leaves to collect some post-it notes and again returns to the surgery.* | Kirsty is able to find the resources she wants for her play. Kirsty uses her developing writing skills in her play. |
| **Kirsty:** I've got some! *(To one of the children in the surgery)* | Kirsty uses talk to inform. |
| **Jack:** You're poorly are you? *(To the observer)* I'm a doctor and a nurse as well. | Jack is confident to engage an adult in his play. Jack and Rory use talk to make their roles clear. |
| **Rory:** I'm a nurse too. | |
| **Jack:** You're really bleeding. She's been bleeding on her arm. You're poorly now. Now you're really poorly. Right I'm bandaging your leg, because you're poorly aren't you. Police register, I've put you on the register. | Jack uses talk to describe what is happening and to describe his actions. Both Jack and Kirsty are trying out new vocabulary, not always accurately but having a go, for example 'police register' and 'optician'. |
| **Kirsty:** You need to come to the optician. What's your name? | |
| *Kirsty examines the adult's arm.* | |
| **Kirsty:** You're not okay, you're not. Where do you hurt? | Kirsty is creating a drama in her play. |
| **Jack:** I've got two pens. We've both got two pens. | Jack and Kirsty converse with each other and there is a flow in their talk and play. |
| **Kirsty:** That's mine! | |
| **Jack:** You have that one. | |
| **Kirsty:** I'm sharing them. | |
| **Jack:** And what is your name again? | |
| **Kirsty:** You have to stay here for lots of your days. If you don't stay here you'll die. | Is Kirsty using dialogue she has heard on television? |
| *Billy joins the surgery role play.* | |
| **Kirsty:** I've got you a drink, okay? | |
| *Jack supports Billy with his writing.* | Jack is applying his literacy skills to support a peer. |
| **Jack:** With a /o/ /o/ /o/. | |
| **Kirsty:** How many have you got, because I've got five? Do you want a drink Rory? | Kirsty keeps the flow of dialogue going by asking questions. |
| **Rory:** No I'm not poorly. | Rory becomes more vocal and finds his way in to the dialogue, gaining confidence. |
| **Kirsty:** Do you want a drink Jack? | |
| **Jack:** I'll have it later. | |
| **Rory:** That was nice doctor. Jack, would you like a drink? | |
| **Jack:** Later, for later, I won't drink it now I said. | |
| *Billy lies down on the floor and Jack attends to him.* | |
| **Jack:** *(To Rory)* You're standing on the bed. *(To the adult)* It's a bed isn't it? | |

## Next steps

- Encourage Rory's engagement in role play where he is becoming increasingly confident in his dialogue with his peers.
- Ask Kirsty and Jack to tell their own stories, scribe their stories and support them to illustrate these and share with others.
- Provide story and non-fiction books about hospitals and visits to the doctors, dentists and opticians to develop the children's knowledge and understanding further.

Figure 6.5: Foundation Stage/Reception class learning story: Rehan

| | |
|---|---|
| Rehan asks me, "Can I have a turn on the computer board?"<br><br>I responded, "Oh, you want a turn on the interactive whiteboard. Here you are!"<br><br>I hand Rehan the clipboard.<br><br>Rehan says, "Look, I write my name like this!" |  |
| Rehan makes marks that represent his name. The 'R' is a recognisable letter.<br><br>I praise Rehan, he shows he wants to write his name and likes to use the clipboard.<br><br>Rehan says, "I have to wait for Arqam to finish. Hurry up Arqam!" |  |
| Rehan reaches up to select the programme he wants.<br>He does this with confidence and pleasure. |  |
| Rehan has selected the Them Bones programme from Education City. He is trying to complete the skeleton by clicking on each bone and dragging it across to the x-ray picture. Rehan finds this tricky and his friend, Arqam, offers some guidance. Eventually Rehan is able to complete the skeleton and the final pieces he has placed independently. |  |
| Rehan stands back to view his achievement.<br><br>"Look at that!", he says.<br><br>"I made the skeleton! I knew I could do it!" |  |

### Analysis of Rehan's learning

- Rehan wanted to write his name and wrote a recognisable 'R'.
- Rehan has persevered to complete the Them Bones game on the interactive whiteboard.
- Rehan likes to play alongside his friends and values their support.

### Next steps

- Does he write anywhere else? Make a note of other times.
- Show Rehan and his friends where the clipboards are kept. I don't think they realise they are transportable.
- Ask Shahnaz to note Rehan's responses to the next few phonics sessions.

# ASSESSING LANGUAGE AND LITERACY ··························

## Figure 6.6: Year 2 learning story: Pamela

<table>
<tr>
<td>
Pamela is comparing two photographs depicting nurses from the past and the present. I have asked the children to look carefully at the two photographs, to compare them and then to write down the differences and similarities between the two.

Pamela writes below the photograph of nurses in the present day.

Tow are hoadin a foada.

Woman and men wurck at hosptl.

Thair werin wite and bleu.

Sum are werin a hat and sum are not werin hat's.

*Two are holding folders.*

*Women and men work at hospital.*

*They are wearing white and blue*

*Some are wearing hats and some are not wearing hats.*
</td>
<td></td>
</tr>
<tr>
<td>
Pamela continues to write below the photograph of nurses from the past.

Thair close are wite. Thair don't have men at hosptl.
Thair not hoadin foddas.

Thair werin yoonifform.

*Their clothes are white. They don't have men at hospital. They are not holding folders.*

*They are wearing uniform.*
</td>
<td></td>
</tr>
<tr>
<td>
Nothing appears to distract Pamela from her writing.
She shows high levels of involvement.
I ask Pamela how are the nurses different in the two photographs.
Pamela informs me, "Because they are wearing hats and some of them are not".
"Those have the cross sign and these don't."
</td>
<td></td>
</tr>
<tr>
<td>
When asked how are the nurses in the two photographs similar, she replies, "Because they are wearing uniforms". And continues,

"Because there are no men in this picture because in the olden days there were no men nurses".
</td>
<td></td>
</tr>
</table>

### Analysis of Pamela's learning

- Pamela can use descriptive language in her writing to make comparisons, identifying both similarities and differences.
- Pamela applies her phonic knowledge when she does not know how to spell a word.

### Next steps

- Give time to Pamela to edit her own work. By revisiting can she self-correct spelling?
- Help Pamela to plan her presentation before she starts writing.
- Provide artefacts from the past and present for the children to compare and write descriptions for a class museum.

**Figure 6.7: Delilah, nursery, 3 years 9 months**

Delilah goes to the art area and selects a rectangular piece of white paper. She applies red paint across the paper and experiments by taking a stick and making vertical and horizontal marks. Delilah decides to select material to stick on top. She chooses different coloured and shaped paper, lollisticks, purple, green, orange and natural coloured sticks.

Delilah takes the adult's pen and makes some marks. She explains, "That one's a baby cross, big cross, medium, little. I can draw a little one up there. How about if I just did one of them like that and two ones like that?"

Delilah describes her actions and gives explanations.

**Figure 6.8: Vlads, Foundation Stage/Reception class, 4 years 6 months**

Vlads decides to draw a picture of his educator Ms Patel. He tells Ms Patel that he has written his name, thus ascribing meaning to the marks he has made. He also makes marks to represent 'Mama!'

# ASSESSING LANGUAGE AND LITERACY

---

### Figure 6.9: Iqra, Foundation Stage/ Reception class, 5 years 5 months

Iqra was asked to write her name and to draw and write about a story.

Iqra decided to illustrate her family and her writing focusses on her dad. She writes, "Dad is in the wheelbarrow".

Iqra is able to form the 'I' correctly in her name and she attempts the other three letters; the 'a' is reversed.

In her sentence writing she uses both upper and lower case letters. "DAD" is clear and although the 's' is reversed, the word "is" is legible.

Iqra is gaining confidence in her ability to write and is beginning to apply what she is learning in phonics sessions.

---

### Figure 6.10: Khurhain, Year 1 class, 5 years 9 months

The children have been enjoying the story of *The Twelve Dancing Princesses*. During independent learning, Khurhain has chosen to access the writing area. She selected a zigzag book and she wrote and illustrated three sentences. Khurhain's writing is legible, most of the letters are accurately formed and every word is spelt correctly. Her three sentences rhyme and they show her confidence in the writing process.

---

## Figure 6.11: Haidar, Year 2 class, 6 years 5 months

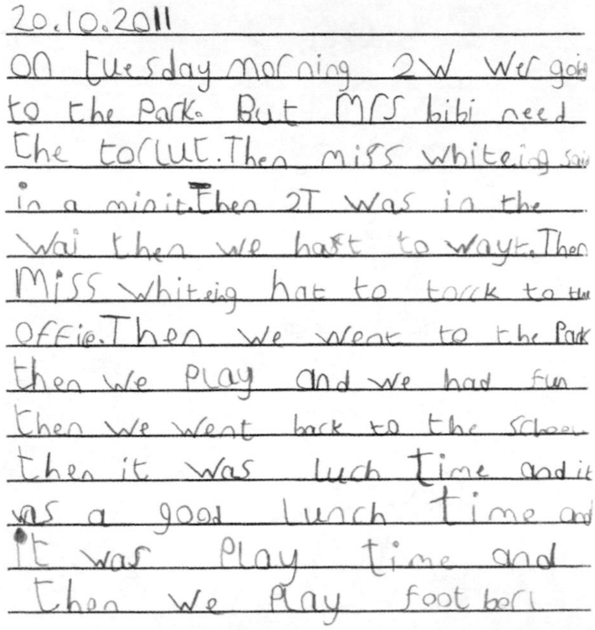

20.10.2011
On tuesday morning 2W wer goin
to the Park. But MrS bibi need
the torlut. Then miss whiteig saie
in a minit. Then 2T was in the
wai then we hart to wayt. Then
MiSS whiteig hat to tork to the
offie. Then we went to the Park
then we play and we had fun
then we went back to the Schoo
then it was luch time and it
was a good lunch time and
it was play time and
then we play footborl

The children have enjoyed the story *In a Minute*[7]. The children in the story are getting ready to go to the park with their family. Every time they ask their parents if they can go, the adults reply, "In a minute". The educators in Year 2 took all the children to a park near the school. They arranged for certain delays to happen before setting off. This was the inspiration for the children's writing, to write an account of their own visit.

Haidar (whose first language is Mirpuri Punjabi) has recently gained confidence in writing. Haidar's account is in sequence and he has successfully used the phrase "in a minute". He spells most words correctly and uses his phonic knowledge when unsure. He self-corrects the spelling of "lunch". Haidar includes some descriptive vocabulary. He punctuates his work, not always correctly. Most importantly of all Haidar achieves the build up of delays before the class eventually leaves for the park.

7   Bradman T, Browne E (2011) *In a Minute*. Second Edition. Frances Lincoln Children's Books, London, UK.

## Figure 6.12: Subhan, Year 2 class, 7 years 3 months

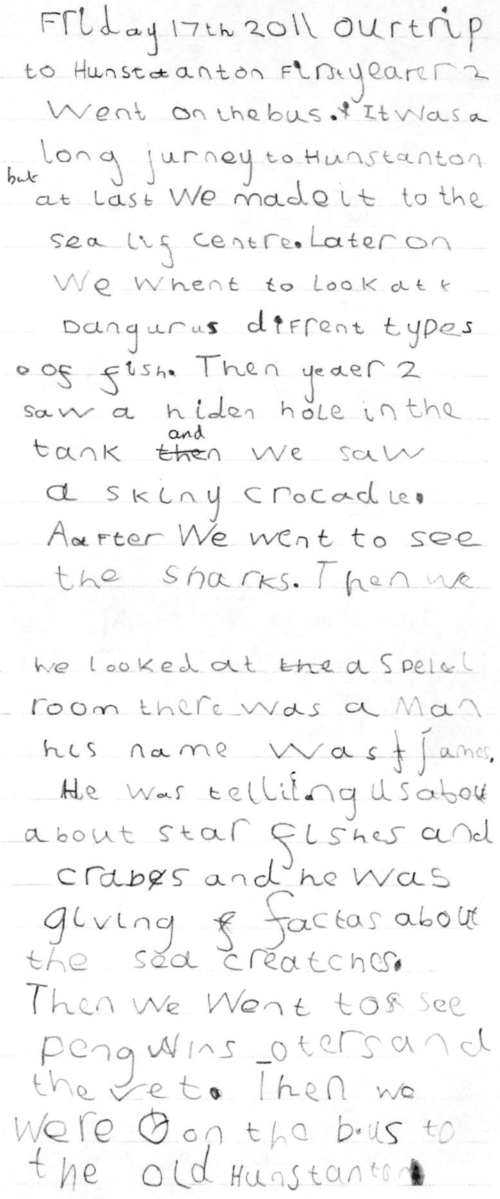

Frlday 17th 2011 ourtrip
to Hunstanton Flnnyearer 2
Went on thebus. It was a
long jurney to Hunstanton
but at last we made it to the
sea lng centre. Later on
We whent to look att
Dangurus diffrent types
of fish. Then year 2
saw a hiden hole in the
tank and then we saw
a skiny crocadie.
Aarter we went to see
the sharks. Then we

we looked at the a spelel
room there was a Man
his name was James.
He was tellilng us abou
about star flshes and
crabes and he was
glving factas abou
the sea creatches.
Then we Went tor see
pengwins otersand
the vet. Then we
were on the bus to
the old Hunstanton

Subhan's class had visited the seaside town of Hunstanton. In Chapter 16 there are examples of how the children planned their writing. Subhan writes a full account of his experience in sequential order. He uses descriptive vocabulary, such as "dangerous different types of fish". Subhan spells the majority of words accurately and makes a good attempt at those he is less familiar with, such as "jurney" and "pengwins". He uses his knowledge of words and phonics to help him. He self-corrects by simply crossing out.

# ASSESSING LANGUAGE AND LITERACY ·····························

**Figure 6.13:** Flo reads *Look at the Pencil* and the educator keeps a running record of her developing reading skills

| Text | Record |
|---|---|
| **Title Page**<br><br>Look at the house | ✓ ✓✓ ✓<br>Look at the house |
| **Page 1**<br><br>"*Look at the roof*",<br><br><br>said the pencil | ✓ ✓✓<br>Look at the rectangle/roof ⟶ (*Flo self-corrects*)<br><br>✓<br>said the pencil (*Educator supports*) |
| **Page 2**<br><br>"*Look at the door*",<br><br><br>said the pencil | ✓ ✓✓ ✓<br>Look at the door (*Flo refers to the picture*)<br>✓ ✓ ✓<br>said the pencil |
| **Page 3**<br><br>"*Look at the windows*",<br><br><br>said the pencil | ✓ ✓✓    ✓<br>Look at the windows<br>✓ ✓ ✓<br>said the pencil |
| **Page 4**<br><br>"*Look at the chimney*",<br><br><br><br>said the pencil | ✓ ✓✓<br>Look at the fence/chimney<br>        (*Educator supports with a context cue from the picture*)<br>✓ ✓ ✓<br>said the pencil |
| **Page 5**<br><br>"*Look at the path*",<br><br><br><br>said the pencil | ✓ ✓ ✓<br>Look at the wall/path<br>        (*Educator supports with a context cue from the picture*)<br>✓ ✓ ✓<br>said the pencil |
| **Page 6**<br><br>"*Look at the fence*",<br><br><br><br>said the pencil | ✓ ✓ ✓<br>Look at the wall/fence<br>        (*Educator supports with a context cue from the picture*)<br>✓ ✓ ✓<br>said the pencil |
| **Page 7**<br><br>"*Look at the gate*",<br><br><br>said the pencil | ✓ ✓ ✓ ✓<br>Look at the gate (*Flo refers to the picture*)<br>✓ ✓ ✓<br>said the pencil |
| **Page 8**<br><br>"*Look at the house*", | ✓ ✓ ✓ ✓<br>Look at the house |

·····················································································

# Texts for reading

The story *The Twelve Dancing Princesses* stimulated some writing

The particular texts that children experience are one of the most important aspects of the teaching of reading[1]. First and foremost, it is essential that children are motivated to read (see Chapter 2) and that they read a sufficient amount. Research has shown, perhaps not surprisingly, that the more children read the better they become as readers[2]. The selection of texts is influenced by two facets of readers' experience: range and depth. It is good for children to experience a range of texts such as: fiction and non-fiction; environmental print; nursery rhymes, songs and poetry; comics, magazines and newspapers. Texts also come increasingly in electronic forms: email and other forms of communication; games; electronic books. The potential range of texts is vast. Perhaps the best solution to this is a combination of texts that children are interested in, and texts selected by educators because of their enthusiasms and because they want to introduce children to new experiences. Many picture books are now extremely sophisticated and thought-provoking. Words and pictures are combined to tell multiple narratives, and there is evidence that children read pictures as well as words[3].

Another major type of text is that written for the express purpose of teaching children. The most popular of these are

1    Meek M (1988) *How Texts Teach What Readers Learn*. Thimble Press, Stroud, UK.

2    Stanovich K (1986) Matthew effects in reading: Some consequences of individual differences in the acquisition of literacy. *Reading Research Quarterly*, 21(4), 360-407.

3    Arizpe E, Styles M (2003) *Children Reading Pictures: Interpreting visual texts*. RoutledgeFalmer, London, UK.

# TEXTS FOR READING

reading schemes (or basals as they call them in the USA). In the past there have been some particularly poor texts that were part of reading schemes, some so poor that they were easy targets for ridicule. However, in general reading scheme texts are now much better than they were. But they cannot offer the same experience that a typical trade book written by an author with the intention of entertaining can offer. One of the reasons for this is that their vocabulary is limited to support the learning of particular words. There is some evidence that the classroom processes supporting the use of these texts can result in some undesirable consequences in relation to children's perceptions of themselves as readers[4].

Assigning reading levels to texts is another feature of reading schemes. But levelling texts is rarely as straightforward as it may appear when reading some explanations of levelling processes. There is, of course, a natural indication of when a text is too hard – when a child simply can't read it. In general children of all ages do make sensible choices about texts when given the chance. There will be a minority who do not, and the educator will need to provide support to help them make more appropriate choices.

Range is one important factor in supporting children's reading, but so is depth. Depth in reading comes through children pursuing their interests. This might be the books of one author and/or books on a particular subject, or re-reading favourite books, each time discovering something new. Educators have to be careful that in their enthusiasm to expose children to a wide range of texts they don't forget the important learning that goes on when children exercise choice.

Young children will express a preference for a favourite text from a very young age. One child, Alice, explained that she liked Bob the Builder[5] because he was on television and she liked his theme tune. Educators who provide texts that reflect popular culture will see that these books draw children to the book area. As Alice looked at the Bob the Builder book she repeatedly sang the theme tune (some of you reading this book may remember it topped the music chart!)

Two useful publications provide lists of books that have had proven success in settings. *The Core Booklist*[6] is published by the Centre for Literacy in Primary Education and the second recommended text, *Early Years Non-fiction*[7], provides guidance for selecting factual texts.

## Reviewing books with seven year olds

The educator asked a group of children to think about different book types. The children's ideas included: joke books, story books, pop-up books, interesting books, information books, non-fiction books, cook books and fiction books. The children were then given time with their talk partners to decide which was their favourite type of book:

"Horrible History[8] books because they are true and they tell you how to make lots of recipes."

"I like fiction books because they are exciting and it has good words and it's funny."

"I like cook books it tells you about everything you like to eat."

"I like Horrible Histories because it tells you what people used to do before all of us were born."

The children were also asked to decide which was their favourite book:

"I like the story called *I Like Books*[9] because it tells you about all sorts of different books you can read and you can buy."

---

4  Levy R (2009) Children's perceptions of reading and the use of reading scheme texts. *Cambridge Journal of Education*, 39(3), 361-377.

5  HIT Entertainment Ltd (2009) *Bob the Builder: Gripper and grabber and the sports stadium* [example of one book in the series]. HIT Entertainment Ltd, London, UK.

6  Centre for Literacy in Primary Education (2010) *The Core Booklist*. Centre for Literacy in Primary Education, London, UK.

7  Mallett M (2003) *Early Years Non-fiction. A guide to helping young researchers use information texts*. RoutledgeFalmer, London, UK.

8  Deary T, Tongue N (1993) *The Terrible Tudors* [example of book in Horrible Histories series]. Scholastic Hippo, London, UK.

9  Browne A (2003) *I Like Books*. Walker Books, London, UK.

Figure 7.1: Artus reviewed *No Ball Games*[13]

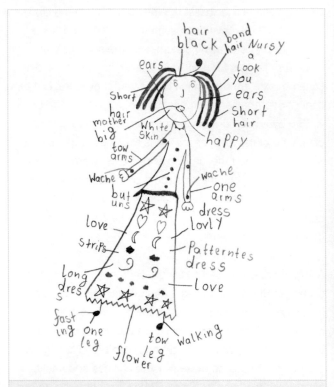

Figure 7.2: Nagina reviewed *Tiger Hunt*[14]. She decided to focus on the appearance of a character

"I like *Charlotte's Web*[10]. Because we had a play of *Charlotte's Web*. And the spider said I'm gonna die and the spider died ... I love that book."

"I like *The Lighthouse Keeper's Lunch*[11] because when the lighthouse keeper gets his food from the cottage the birds start eating it. Then they put mustard inside it so they go to a different person, the fisherman."

"I like *Horrid Henry*[12] books because he is really naughty to his family and Horrid Henry is a little bit funny. I wouldn't be like Horrid Henry because I might get into trouble."

"I like *The Terrible Tudors* book because they tell you about recipes for terrible food but they're really nice."

Writing book reviews is a good way to enable children to reflect on and write about the different aspects of a book, such as the storyline, the characters and the setting. However it is important to remember that oral discussion focussed on reviewing books, perhaps like adult book groups, is very valuable. Writing book reviews should be done when the educator intends the writing to be a focus of teaching. Occasionally a more ambitious reviewing focus might include the development of a class book prize, including 'authors' interviewed by the media, and panel members selecting short-lists and then voting.

In the book reviews shown in Figures 7.1 to 7.3, the children, aged seven, have chosen the books for review themselves. They worked independently and reviewed the books pictorially.

10  White E B (2003) *Charlotte's Web*. Puffin Books, London, UK.

11  Armitage D, Armitage R (1994) *The Lighthouse Keeper's Lunch*. Scholastic Hippo, London, UK.

12  Simon F (1994) *Horrid Henry*. Orion Publishing Group, London, UK.

13  Akass S (2000) *No Ball Games* (Rigby Star Guided series). Pearson, London, UK.

14  Waite J (2000) *Tiger Hunt* (Rigby Star Guided series). Pearson, London, UK.

# TEXTS FOR READING

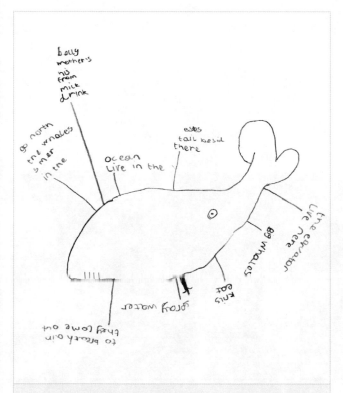

Figure 7.3: Umair reviewed *Big Blue, Little Blue*[15]. He decided to find out facts about whales from the story

## Responding to children's reading choices

Educators often plan specific activities and learning experiences to develop children's understanding of stories. Core books[16] are those that are selected by early years educators because they know they will support children's intrinsic motivation to read.

As part of long term planning it is a good idea to identify a number of texts that will be experienced in more depth throughout the year. The number of core books is dependent on the previous experience of the children and where stories sit within the whole setting and school Literacy and English policies. A focus on one core book does not exclude the

experience of other stories, and revisiting favourites is an important part of children's learning.

When identifying core books and non-fiction texts as part of long term planning for early years children, it is important to have criteria to ensure a balance of texts.

Considerations include:

- A balance of stories that portray animals and 'real' people as characters

- A balance between traditional tales, favourite texts such as *The Very Hungry Caterpillar*[17] and contemporary stories

- A balance between boy and girl heroes

- A balance between texts from different cultural perspectives.

Here's an example of how a team of educators used planning for core books in response to their concern that too many girls in Year 1 were not as engaged in their learning as the boys. The educators decided to select a core story that would be appealing to girls, and that they could support with role play, small world play and with dressing up: they chose *The Twelve Dancing Princesses*[18].

A castle role play became an important focal point. Both boys and girls enjoyed dressing up as the different characters: the grumpy king, the princesses, the maid, Prince Marcus and Jasper the magician. The quality of the provision motivated the children's engagement with the text.

---

15  Doyle M (2000) *Big Blue, Little Blue* (Rigby Star Guided series). Pearson, London, UK.

16  Shell R (1992) *Language Works: Language and literacy development in the multi-lingual classroom*. Tower Hamlets Education, London, UK.

17  Carle E (2002) *The Very Hungry Caterpillar*. New Edition. Puffin Books, London, UK.

18  Davidson S, Luraschi A (2007) *The Twelve Dancing Princesses* [based on the fairytale by The Brothers Grimm]. Usbourne Picture Books, London, UK.

# The learning environment for reading

Sharing books in comfortable surroundings develops a love for books and reading

We suggested in Chapter 7 that texts are at the heart of reading teaching. Children need to have as many opportunities as possible to select and engage with texts. This means that the storage and presentation of texts is important. But before the texts are stored the educator needs sufficient knowledge of the best kinds of texts to acquire and use. In addition to initial teacher training and continuing professional development opportunities, there is a range of ways in which knowledge about texts can be developed. A specialist book supplier or a knowledgeable librarian can be

ideal. Children's literature prize lists can provide inspiration and there are numerous books[1] and websites which help educators learn about the range of books available.

There need to be opportunities for children to access texts in different ways. This means that the environment of the classroom needs to be set up to engage children with literacy. One particularly important element is the reading area where the books are stored and displayed, where children can browse, make selections, share with their peers,

---

1   Hahn D, Flynn L, Reuben S (eds) (2004) *The Ultimate Book Guide*. A&C Black, London, UK (available from www.justimaginestorycentre.co.uk/).

# THE LEARNING ENVIRONMENT FOR READING

and where adults can interact in more informal ways to take children's reading forward. Reading areas are normally comfortable spaces with books appropriately stored and displayed for easy access. The book supply should include books made by children. Comics and magazines need to be changed regularly as they are not as robust as books. Electronic devices also increasingly provide opportunities for convenient storage of a large number of texts. It is also important to remember that the walls and other surfaces of the learning environment provide spaces for imaginative, informative and thought-provoking displays of texts.

In addition to the provision of resources, there is a range of routines that support reading. The planning of educator-directed reading activities is one important routine that we illustrate in the second half of this chapter. Reading aloud a wide range of texts including non-fiction, and singing or playing games with children are daily occurrences. Reading aloud from a class reader is a timeless activity that can both motivate and challenge children to think differently. Special collections of books can be rotated around classes in schools: for example, collections of poetry books that augment the examples in the classroom reading area, or themed collections that include related artefacts. Book packs that include props such as small world figures or puppets linked with the particular books in the pack can add to children's enjoyment. Settings also need routines to enable books to be taken home to be shared with family members, and for comments to be written into reading diaries.

Routines for reading include whole class, small group and one-to-one reading. Whole class reading teaching includes not only the opportunity for dramatic story readings and tellings, but also the opportunity for discussion. The nature of educator-pupil interaction is an important contributor to learning (see Chapter 4)[2]. Two of the most important facets of high quality teacher-pupil interaction are the encouragement of extended dialogue by children with the educator and with their peers, and ensuring a variety of types of interaction that includes open questions, provocative statements, and encouragement to voice informed opinions. Small group reading can encourage the shared construction of ideas about the same text. Children with similar needs can also on

## Box 8.1: Benefits of reading and rereading

It benefits children to see texts before they are used in planned lessons and also to have those books to refer to long after the theme has been covered. Children need to become very familiar with texts, something that does not happen for all children within a week, so access over the year is important. Space can become an issue so as themes are covered, it can be agreed between the educators and the children which texts will remain readily available, and which will be stored.

occasion be brought together to jointly learn a new skill or develop new understanding. One-to-one reading is also a powerful teaching opportunity that we cover in Chapter 10.

The provision of an exciting book area in the early years setting is vital to developing the children's intrinsic motivation to read. Children will be drawn to familiar texts (see Box 8.1 on the benefits of reading and rereading) and props that enhance their enjoyment of them. So starting with what children already know and enjoy is key.

## An inspiring book area for three year olds

Do not forget to start with the children's interests and known literary favourites. The book area needs to include the following:

- Selection of carefully selected high quality story books

- Selection of high quality non-fiction texts that build on and extend the children's interests

- Posters depicting books and their authors

- Comfortable seating to enable children to share books with an adult. A sofa is ideal (if space permits) because this provides a familiar physical link with home

---

2   Mercer N (2008) The seeds of time: Why classroom dialogue needs a temporal analysis. *Journal of the Learning Sciences*, 17(1), 33-59.

Five year olds access the book area

Three year olds access the book area

- Floor cushions: for many children it is their preference to look at books lying or sitting on the floor

- Props to enrich the children's enjoyment of the story books, such as book characters as soft toys

- Prompts for adults: suggestions to get dialogue started to support less confident adults

- A listening area which includes a digital player with headphones to enable the children to listen to stories independently. A listening area also provides the opportunity for stories to be heard in a range of different languages.

If there is an interactive whiteboard in the setting, children can be further motivated when they see their favourite story on a DVD and projected onto the screen.

If the setting does not have access to a school library, regular visits to the local library can encourage families to join and ensure their children have access to so many more book choices.

## An inspiring book area for six year olds

The principle of high quality story and non-fiction books also applies for six year olds. However, the range needs to be greater to meet the needs of all the children in the class. The identification and development of children's interests needs to be on-going. Include the following in the book area:

- Story books from Year 1, particularly in the first half of the autumn term to support transition to Year 2. If core stories have been selected, for example six texts for the year, then they all need to be in the book area, preferably with multiple copies.

- Non-fiction books that support all the themes to be covered during the academic year.

- The children's favourite books: there is nothing better than seeing your favourite book to pick up and read.

A five-year-old child initiates
reading the rhyme *Two Little Dicky Birds*

Figures 8.1 and 8.2 show two observations which exemplify the educator's role in following the children's cues. It is equally important for the educator to plan opportunities for adult-directed reading activities.

Educators reading to children one to one, in small groups and whole class groups, inspires the children's participation in these planned opportunities which include the following:

- Creating a story setting in small world play and the children retelling the story using the props.

- Creating a story setting in role play areas inside and outside. Children can refer to the text as they drama role play the story.

- Non-fiction texts are ideally placed in different areas of provision, so books about fish work well in the water area (make them waterproof first), books about vehicles in the sand area and books specifically about maths and science complement the maths and investigative areas of the provision.

- Educators can plan an activity to go alongside each area of provision. A book about fish can inspire accurate fish identification and a book about building vehicles can motivate the children to learn more about what each vehicle does.

- Specific sentences, phrases and words can be highlighted on laminated card so that children can carry them around, and take them to the writing areas for more extension work.

- Sharing sets of books in small groups so that every child has a book to hold and use. Supporting a group of six children, it is possible to let every child read simultaneously, focussing on one child at a time.

- Reading one to one allows the educator to maintain a running record and provide better informed support for each child.

- Books produced by the children themselves: this is a good link with the class writing area where provision for book-making can be an excellent motivator for writing.

- Books produced by either older children in the school or children from a nearby school.

- Books produced by parents and carers: family literacy groups are a good place for different types of books to be produced, such as a family recipe book.

- A display board to feature children's book reviews.

At the right stage (perhaps age six or seven) children should also have access to the school library on a regular basis. They can learn how the library is organised and become accomplished at finding the books they want on the library computers using software such as Junior Librarian[3].

When a planned learning opportunity works repeat that strategy in a range of contexts. Props and laminated resources should be efficiently stored and accessible at any time so that educators can immediately follow up the children's strengths, needs and interests.

3   Junior Librarian software, Clas4Schools (available from www.clas4schools.com/junior_librarian.html).

Figure 8.1: Child observation in an early years setting: three year olds reading in the book area

| Child's name: Sam  Child's age: 3 years 6 months | Child's name: Lily  Child's age: 3 years 9 months |
|---|---|
| Date of observation: 15th October 2011 | Time and length of observation: 2.30pm, 10 minutes |
| Location: Book area | Keyworker: Catherine |

### Description

I went to sit in the book area to see if any of the children would be interested in looking at the books. Just by sitting in the area, Sam soon came to join me. He was looking at one book and then asked me to read it to him. As soon as I started to read the story Lily came to join us. Sam and Lily enjoyed talking about the different trucks illustrated in the book. Lily said, "Look, that book's Dora, I love Dora! I've got a Dora puzzle at home. I'm gonna read that one. Watch me!" Lily confidently selected the *Dora the Explorer*[4] book. Lily reads aloud, starting at the beginning of the book, turning each page in turn, making up her own story. Sam was more interested in describing the building trucks in great detail. He informed me, "This one is really important. It moves all the rocks and rubbish. Have you seen one of these?"

**Note:** Photograph taken

### Reflections

Both Sam and Lily responded positively to an adult being in the area. This prompt helped them to be more engaged in books and listening to stories as well as making meaning for themselves from the illustrations. Sam liked to point out different pictures and ask questions.

### Next steps

- Tell parents about favourite books.

- Suggest children might like to take these books home.

### Parent/s comment/s

Sam's father: We didn't realise Sam was so interested in books. I am going to make the effort to take him to the library.

Lily's mother: She likes Dora the Explorer best.

---

4   Nickelodeon (2010) *Dora's 10 Best Adventures*. Simon and Schuster Children's Books, London, UK.

# THE LEARNING ENVIRONMENT FOR READING ············

Figure 8.2: Child observation in an early years setting: five year olds reading in the book area

| | |
|---|---|
| **Child's name:** Asma  **Child's age:** 5 years 3 months | **Child's name:** Laila  **Child's age:** 5 years 7 months |
| **Date of observation:** 6th October 2011 | **Length of observation:** 10 minutes |
| **Location:** Book area in the Year 1 classroom | **Keyworker:** Sanum |

**Description**

Asma and Laila invited me into the book area to read our core story *The Twelve Dancing Princesses*. Asma and Laila listened to the whole story and then they wanted me to read it again. On the second reading they both began to join in with familiar parts of the text. In the part of the story where the characters sail across the lake Asma said, "I know that word! It's castle, like Castle Rising. I know that 'cos I writted it". Laila pointed to the word 'bobbed'; "what's that, it looks like 'bob' like 'Bob the Builder'. I'm gonna sound talk. /b/ /o/ /b/ /e/ /d/ bobbed, bobbed? What's that". I explained the meaning of 'bob' and 'bobbing up and down'. We bobbed up and down in the book area.

At the scene where the princesses dance at the wedding, Asma said, "I can read 'Jasper' because Mrs Harrap asked us about our best characters and I said Jasper".

**Note:** Photograph taken

**Reflections**

Asma and Laila have memorised this story. They are beginning to want to read some of it. Asma could read "once", "castle" and "Jasper". Laila could read "king". They both read "seen and not heard" and "sleep tight".

**Next steps**

- Present the children with extracts of the text to read. Provide them with the opportunity to create their own version.

- Give a choice of how they could do this, for instance a zigzag book or a story map.

- Remind Asma and Laila of their new word 'bobbed'. See if we can create the scene in the water tray.

**Parent/s comment/s**

Asma's mother: Asma doesn't stop talking about this story. She is always dressing up as one of the princesses. She likes dancing around the room. She makes me laugh.

# Children's names

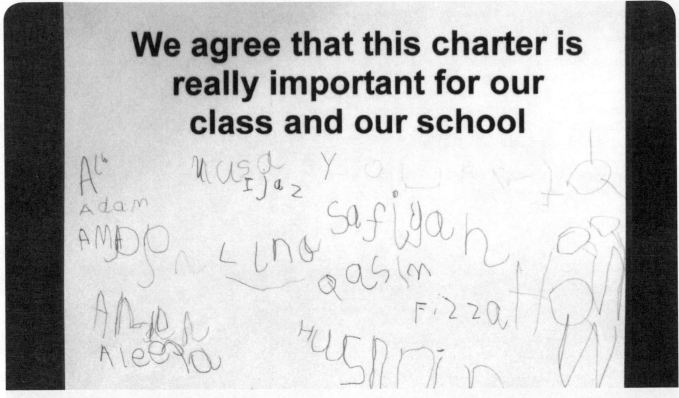

**We agree that this charter is really important for our class and our school**

The children have written their names to show they have signed up for the class charter

Children's names are some of the most important words that they encounter. First and foremost they are an essential part of their identity. The ability to name each other is one of the many aspects that makes humans different from animals. Children's names are typically the first words that they encounter in reading and writing. They also offer a myriad of possibilities for learning. Janet Bloodgood[1] showed how name-writing was linked to a range of important early literacy learning. Links were found between name-writing and learning of the alphabetic code, although individual children differed in the extent to which they could form letters and/or name letters. It was theorised that learning the alphabetic code and name-writing reinforced each other, and it was noted that this learning occurred in an integrated way in the early years settings that were studied.

Names are in one sense very simple: they identify people. But as linguistic elements they are profound and complex. Names have whole histories behind them, passed down as they are through the generations. Some names such as "Plumb" have modern meanings (Mr Plumb is a real plumber who did some work for Dominic!) Other names have meanings that stretch back to antiquity. Names are of course also words. The young child has to develop understanding of what a word is. They will first encounter words orally as part of continuous speech streams. But they will also need to learn that in printed language words are separated by spaces. A name is also a particular form of noun that requires a capital letter. Here links can be made with learning about the two cases of the alphabet.

1   Bloodgood J (1999) What's in a name? Children's name writing and literacy acquisition. *Reading Research Quarterly*, 34(3), 342-367.

# CHILDREN'S NAMES

Names as words can be broken down into syllables. It is ironic that in spite of their ubiquity they are some of the most complex phonologically. Consider the phoneme to letter correspondences for names such as: Ainé; John; Bryn; Esther; Shaida. Names are an important source for learning about the complex reality of the links between phonemes and letters.

Names are also the first words that children attempt to write, often with family members' support. Children tend to include the letters from their name more frequently in mark-making in the early stages. Much useful work on holding writing implements and forming letters appropriately can be done with the writing of names. When helping children to write their name, using the real names of letters (A-B-C) to refer to letters, and making a clear distinction between these letter names and the phonemes that they represent, contributes to understanding of the alphabetic code[2].

## Working with children's names in the early years setting

Within the early years setting promoting children's awareness of their name is a daily occurrence. Children arrive at the beginning of the session and register themselves. To do this they find their name and place it on the class chart or put it in a basket or container. During this short interlude, children frequently compare their name with their friends' names. This comparison includes identifying letters that are the same and those that are different.

Placing name cards in writing areas stimulates the children to experiment with name-writing. They soon want to write their own name on paintings, pictures and models to show their ownership. Initially educators encourage whatever marks the child makes to represent their own name. From seeing their name in a range of contexts children naturally realise that they can write their name conventionally. Educators can then build on children's interests to help them form letters appropriately and understand that a name is a word.

### Figure 9.1: A form that encourages children to write their names

| Did you walk to pre-school today? | Yes | No |
|---|---|---|
| Christine | ✓ | |
| | | |
| | | |
| | | |
| | | |

The child's writing of their own name is further developed by providing forms, greetings cards and registers to fill in. Role play areas should be rich with these opportunities, and children will know where to find their name to copy, as and when they need to. Role play outside can be enhanced with passports and driving licences to provide further practice within a meaningful context.

Educators also plan tasks that require children to write their name. For example, props and pictures displayed on a low table can be accompanied with questions that invite children to write their names (see Figure 9.1).

A different question can be posed each day, for example:

- Did you come to pre-school/school in a car?

- Did you come to pre-school/school in a taxi?

- Did you come to pre-school/school by bus?

- Did you come to pre-school/school in a rocket?

---

2   Treiman R, Pennington B, Shriberg D, Boada R (2008) Which children benefit from letter names in learning letter sounds? *Cognition*, 106, 1322-1338.

# Strategies for reading

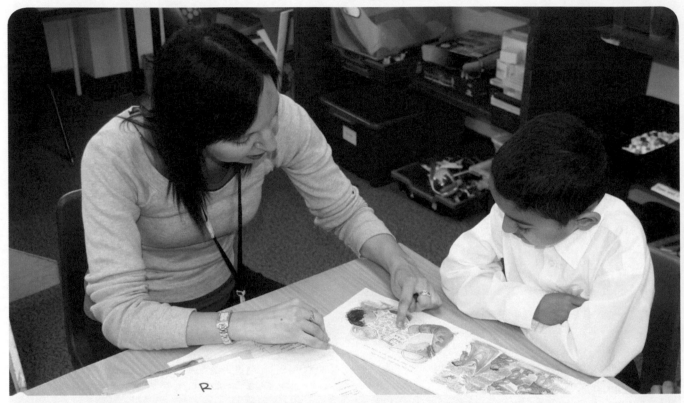

Reading one to one with an educator

The educator's ability to interact with a small group or a whole class can be greatly enhanced if they understand the subtleties of reading with an individual child. The supportive, personal context of one-to-one reading is very important. The strategy provides a natural link with the kinds of reading that many children experience at home with parents and other family members. In addition, if educators are to advise parents on effective ways of working with their children, then they need to be knowledgeable and effective at one-to-one reading themselves. One-to-one reading is also important because of its significant value to struggling readers[1]. Educators who work with struggling readers themselves or who delegate this responsibility to teaching assistants need to fully understand the possibilities of one-to-one reading.

The term 'shared reading' or 'shared read' is now associated with a whole class lesson which features a text that a whole class can read, either one that is enlarged electronically or a big book. However, the original 'shared book experience' was developed by Don Holdaway in 1979[2] as a one-to-one experience. The following example is indicative. The extract is from a shared reading session that took place over a period of approximately five minutes, which ended with the educator and the child discussing the story for a few minutes more and the child talking about her own pet's adventures. Five-year-old Kirsty was sharing a new book with her educator. First, the educator read the story while Kirsty looked at the pictures. Then they read through the story again with the educator asking Kirsty questions that drew her

---

1    Clay M (1979) *The Early Detection of Reading Difficulties*. Third Edition. Heinemann Education, Auckland, New Zealand.

2    Holdaway D (1979) *The Foundations of Literacy*. Ashton Scholastic, London, UK.

The Early Literacy Handbook

into conversation about different incidents in the story. Then, when the educator felt Kirsty was ready, she asked her to read aloud:

| | |
|---|---|
| **Educator:** | Your turn to read it, All right, let's see. |
| **Kirsty:** | The dog sees a box. |
| **Educator:** | Mmmh. |
| **Kirsty:** | He sniffs in the box. |
| **Educator:** | He sniffs it, doesn't he? |
| **Kirsty:** | He kicks the box. He climbs in the box. |
| **Educator:** | Oh, now what happens? |
| **Kirsty:** | He falls down the stairs. |
| | The dog falls out the box. The (*Hesitates*). |
| **Educator:** | The (*Pauses*). |
| **Kirsty:** | The dog falls over. |
| **Educator:** | He does, doesn't he? |
| | Then what does he try to do? |

**Original text:**
The dog sees the box.
The dog sniffs the box.
The dog kicks the box.
The dog gets in the box. The dog gets out of the box.
The dog falls over.[3]

Although Kirsty was not reading every word accurately, the meaning of the text had largely been retained, so the educator did not correct the child, although she did make several interjections to support and encourage Kirsty's reading. When the child hesitated, the educator simply restarted the sentence, then paused, prompting Kirsty to respond appropriately. Such one-to-one interactions can effectively take place with all levels and ages of children learning to read. At later stages the educator may be more directive in their support for decoding. The level of text will also change, but the principles of encouragement, support, discussion, instruction and enjoyment will not.

One-to-one sessions are invaluable for assessing children's reading and can help with the identification of struggling readers. A one-to-one session is an ideal opportunity to assess a child's comprehension and understanding of a text, their ability to decode words, and any problems in these

areas. If the educators aim to read individually with every child in their class regularly (at least once per term and more frequently for children aged four and five), this provides an important element of their assessment of children's learning.

As children's reading becomes more fluent, the priorities for one-to-one reading change.

For the majority of children, efficient use of educators' time can be made by gradually moving towards more emphasis on group reading. Overall there is less of a need for one-to-one sessions for fluent readers. However, this does not mean that they should be completely abandoned. The one-to-one session with fluent readers allows for a more in-depth exploration of children's understanding of and response to particular texts. One of the most important things that can be discovered by talking to a child about their reading in the one-to-one session is their motivation for reading. Do they read for pleasure? If so, what kinds of texts are they interested in?

One consideration for the educator is where in the setting the reading might take place. In early years settings and classrooms a comfortable place, where the child feels safe and secure, works well. Soft furnishings, such as sofas and floor cushions, create a comfortable space for sharing books. If reading takes place at a table then it needs to be located in a place where the child is unlikely to be distracted and the educator and child are able to sit side by side. In some schools opportunities for reading are located in other spaces outside the busy classroom. Creating a reading space outside the classroom shows how much this activity is valued. Library spaces are also important and need to provide different spaces for reading.

The opportunities provided for reading indoors and outdoors include educators referring to words in the environment (such as labels, posters, and names) throughout the day. Talking about books and text is not limited to the time for one-to-one reading or group reading sessions. A range of contexts provides opportunities for talking about reading and texts. Educators use specific language to support this: "Look here's a sign for us to read!; I wonder what this says; Here's an interesting letter; Today you have a school newsletter to put in your book bags, let's read it and find out what's happening in the other year groups".

3   Campbell R (1990) *Reading Together*. Open University Press, Buckingham, UK, pp 29-30.

# Interpreting texts

Children enjoy a picture book. Their favourite teddies are included in the storytelling session

Children are naturally predisposed to make sense of life, and this includes making sense of texts. This meaning-making has been explained at the socio-cultural level as a transaction between text and reader: "an event involving a particular individual and a particular text, happening at a particular time, under particular circumstances, in a particular social and cultural setting, and as part of the ongoing life of the individual and the group"[1]. At the cognitive level this is explained as reading comprehension. Where the two perspectives have something in common is in the idea that interpretation of texts requires the ability to extract and construct meaning[2].

There is evidence that explicit teaching of comprehension is important[3]. A number of strategies have been identified that support children's reading comprehension in the hands of skilful educators. These include:

- Summarising texts

- Children generating questions about texts

- Clarifying meanings

- Children verifying their predictions by analysing texts

1   Rosenblatt L (1985) Viewpoints: Transaction versus interaction: A terminological rescue operation. *Research in the Teaching of English*, 19(1), 96-107 [see p 100].

2   Snow C E, Sweet A P (2003) Reading for comprehension. In A P Sweet, C E Snow (eds) *Rethinking Reading Comprehension*. Guilford Press, New York, USA.

3   National Institute of Child Health and Human Development (2000) *Report of the National Reading Panel: Teaching children to read: An evidence-based assessment of the scientific research literature on reading and its implications for reading instruction*. US Government Printing Office, Washington DC, USA.

# INTERPRETING TEXTS

- Summarising

- Visualising scenes

- Using context clues in the text to support discussion about issues related to the text

- Linking texts with children's background knowledge

- Distinguishing main issues from minor issues.

When these strategies are combined, they seem to be more effective than when they are used in isolation.

Picture books offer children a unique opportunity to connect with the author's imaginary world. This can be a particularly intense experience that allows for many possible interpretations of meanings. The features of books that generate such experiences include a stimulating text and arresting illustrations. The best picture books have illustrations which themselves often contain a number of sub-plots. For example, when Lily (in *Lily Takes a Walk*[4]) takes a seemingly peaceful walk, her dog is shown being frightened by a range of bizarre visions conjured by ordinary features of the urban landscape. Arizpe and Styles[5] carried out some research to investigate how children respond to the pictures in this and some other classic picture books. When asked what they expected the book to be about by looking at the front cover, the children said things like: "You think, 'What's the dog scared of?' So you, like, turn the page and then look and then just carry on reading and there's some more monsters and you just want to see the rest of it". The book has A Spooky Surprise Book as part of the front cover, but the cartoon-like illustrations and facial expressions hint at something funny. This is why the children's views varied between expecting a funny book and a scary book. This ambiguity is a deliberate device created by the author to foster children's thinking.

The researchers also asked the children about the dual plot of the book:

**Researcher:** Do you think the pictures are telling the same story as the words?

**Selma:** Yes, plus a bit more ... [the pictures] seem to bring out the story.

In conclusion, the researchers found that children aged 4–11 in their study responded in sophisticated ways to the pictures in the books. The children "read colours, borders, body language, framing devices, covers, endpapers, visual metaphors and visual jokes", and "most children were keen to discuss the moral, spiritual and environmental issues [the pictures] raised".

## Dear Zoo: a core story for children aged three

*Dear Zoo* by Rod Campbell[6] is a popular choice as a core story for young children. The refrain of the book is: I wrote to the zoo to send me a pet. They sent me a ... lion. The children respond to the idea in the book of writing to the zoo to get a pet animal. They like to guess what the different animals could be that are sent on each day of the week. Each animal is hidden behind a flap and this invites physical as well as oral interaction. Children soon understand how the story works. The repeated phrases, "So they sent me a ..."; "He was too ..."; and "I sent him back", are soon learned by the children. When an adult shares the book one to one with a child they can point out the text in the illustration, for example on the labels of the animal containers.

Having read the story several times (one to one and in groups with the keyworker), the educators use the story in different ways to consolidate the children's understanding. Opportunities are provided for the children to invent their own version of the story. In one setting the children wrote to a local zoo themselves and were thrilled to receive a reply. Small world play can be prepared to represent the different animals and the containers, something which invites the children to retell the story for themselves. In the book area, information texts and books are provided to show the animals in their natural habitat.

---

4    Kitamura S (1987) *Lily Takes a Walk*. Picture Corgi, London, UK.

5    Arizpe E, Styles M (2003) *Children Reading Pictures: Interpreting visual texts*. RoutledgeFalmer, London, UK, p 57.

6    Campbell R (1982) *Dear Zoo*. Puffin Books, London, UK.

Eventually the children are ready to create their own story, either individually or as a group activity. For example a large scale format such as a big book, or an electronic form such as PowerPoint, can be used. The children might create the illustrations, and the educators scribe the text based on the children's ideas.

## Silly Billy[7]: a core story for children aged five

As so many stories for young children have animal and fairy tale characters, it is important to balance this with core books that feature a child as the main character. Anthony Browne's story about a boy who worries enables educators to focus on children's empathy and emotional well-being. Browne's illustrations are a mixture of realism and surrealism which powerfully engage children's curiosity.

Billy worries about hats, shoes, clouds, rain, giant birds and about staying at other people's houses. His grandmother comes to his rescue by introducing him to her South American worry dolls. This is not the end to his worries as he worries that he has transferred all his worries onto the dolls. Resolution comes when he decides to make a worry doll for every doll! Educators can either scribe the child's suggestions for the worry dolls or children can write them for themselves. Educators who have shared this story with young children have found that months later the children will remember it and better articulate their own dilemmas.

The book works well because children are not overwhelmed by too much text and, like most high quality picture books, because there is subtle use of repetition, for example through particular phrases. Activities that focus on interpretation of meanings, such as the kinds of worries that children have, precede attention to the smaller units of the text. Repeating phrases that children often naturally learn from memory can be a good starting point. For example, if we take the phrase,

"Billy worried about ... ", 'worry' can be a tricky word for children, semantically and phonetically. Starting at text level, as we have suggested, then proceeding to word level helps the children to better understand such words.

The children can soon invent stories based on their own worries, sharing with their talk partner first and then in small groups. These are further extended by changing the story characters. Who will they tell their worries to? Maybe an adult at school, maybe an adult from their extended family. Children develop their stories and independently create their own version of Silly Billy. The wide use of IT means that educators can either scribe children's ideas which can be seen in print or on screen, and the children can be supported to mark-make themselves. On occasion the educator will take the work through to class-made books that become 'published' for all in the class to share.

In most areas of the setting a copy of the core book is provided for continuous reference. Home corner role play is important for young children up to five, so providing the opportunity to re-enact the original story and children's variations of it is important for extending the children's confidence with words that express emotions and feelings. Children also learn how to make worry dolls so that when engaged in self-initiated learning they can develop their understanding further. These dolls are then provided in the small world play area. As an extension the educator introduces the challenge of building suitable homes for the worry doll families.

This core book would be a focus for one to two weeks. Over the half term educators focus on other stories by Anthony Browne. Children respond positively to this strategy of featuring one author over several weeks. They become familiar with a writer's style. Other children's authors whose books work well in this way include Julia Donaldson, author of the Gruffalo[8] stories, Eric Carle who wrote The Very Hungry Caterpillar, Jill Murphy[9] and her stories about the Bear family and Eileen Browne, the author of Handa's Surprise[10] and, with Tony Bradman, Through My Window[11].

---

7    Browne A (2006) Silly Billy. Walker Books, London, UK.

8    Donaldson J (Scheffler A, illustrator) (1999) The Gruffalo. Macmillan Children's Books, London, UK.

9    Murphy J (1980) Peace at Last. Macmillan Children's Books, London, UK.

10   Browne E (1994) Handa's Surprise. Walker Books, London, UK.

11   Bradman T and Browne E (1986; new edition 2008) Through My Window. Frances Lincoln Children's Books, London, UK.

CHAPTER 12

# Teaching letters and phonemes

Singing outdoors and developing confidence with phonemes

Teaching about the alphabetic code should take place for most children when they are aged five or six. Prior to that time work will have been done on developing the children's phonological awareness and helping children understand some of the features of the letters of the alphabet. The alphabet is one of the greatest human inventions and is a highly sophisticated and efficient system of communication[1]. With good teaching children learn to understand its complexities. Here is one example of why the alphabet is complex: is 'I' a capital letter, the number 1 or the lower case of letter 'L'? The computer keyboard does distinguish: the lower case 'L' is narrower than the capital 'I', and the number 1 has a serif. The capital letter 'I' is also a word, and a word that sounds the same as another word: eye.

The other parts of the complexity include answers to the following questions: what is a capital letter and when should it be used?; what is the sequence of alphabetic order? (very nicely helped by using alphabet songs, wall displays, dictionaries, etc); and of course, how do letters represent sounds and words?

Research has shown that the most effective phonics teaching is contextualised teaching. This means that the learning of phonemes is contextualised in the sentences of whole texts. For most children, age five is the most appropriate time to ensure that systematic teaching about phonemes takes place, but this should be within the context of a whole text[2]. Whole text teaching does not mean that

1   Harris R (1986) *The Origin of Writing*. Duckworth, London, UK.

Finding hidden words from a treasure chest
provides an element of anticipation

Can a chip be thick?
Using 'th' words in a meaningful context

referring to sounds and letters in a decontextualised way is never appropriate but it does mean that most of the teaching should be contextualised. 'Systematic' means a well-planned sequence of teaching of phonemes and letters and their relationship to words, sentences and whole texts. Table 12.1 shows a possible sequence for teaching of graphemes and phonemes.

Phonics teaching should be daily, brief, and the total phonics programme should not go on for too long. The question of how long the programme should go on for is difficult to answer because research has shown effective phonics teaching over quite diverse timescales[3]. Our view is that for most children three months of at most 15 minutes per day should be sufficient.

There is clear evidence that children differ in the nature of phonics teaching that they require[4]. For example, some children will be able to decode straightforward texts at age five and a minority may have been able to do this as young as three[5]. These children do not require systematic phonics teaching. Most children will find the duration of phonics teaching described earlier enough to help them learn to decode. A minority of children will struggle beyond this time and will require one-to-one teaching to help them. This one-to-one teaching should still be contextualised in whole texts.

Prior to teaching graphemes and phonemes through taught daily sessions, educators will have engaged children in a range of learning opportunities that develop:

2   Wyse D, Goswami U (2008) Synthetic phonics and the teaching of reading. *British Educational Research Journal*, 34(6), 691-710.

3   Wyse D (2010) Contextualised phonics teaching. In K Hall, U Goswami, C Harrison, S Ellis, J Soler (eds) *Interdisciplinary Perspectives on Learning to Read: Culture, cognition and pedagogy*. Routledge, London, UK.

4   Connor C M, Piasta S B, Fishman B J, Glasney S, Schatschneider C, Crowe E, Underwood P, Morrison F J (2009) Individualizing student instruction precisely: Effects of child x instruction interactions on first graders' literacy development. *Child Development*, 80(1), 77-100.

5   Wyse D (2007) *How to Help Your Child Read and Write*. Pearson Education Limited, London, UK.

# TEACHING LETTERS AND PHONEMES

- Their confidence to participate in role play

- Their use of talk in a variety of contexts

- Their listening skills, including auditory discrimination

- Their enjoyment of songs and rhymes

- Their confidence in retelling traditional and contemporary stories

- A growing understanding of print, both in the environment and in books

- Their mark-making and emergent writing.

Engaging the children's parents in sharing rhymes, songs, poems and chants with their own children was described in Chapter 2. Rhyme times develop children's confidence in playing with language and help them to understand that all the adults also have an enthusiasm for words. Book Start[6] provides useful advice on how to plan and implement a 'rhyme challenge'. Having a rhyme time challenge on an annual basis raises the profile and value of rhymes in the setting.

When children are developmentally ready for phonics teaching, they will already be recognising their own names and those of their friends and writing their names. They will be able to distinguish, orally, between the different phonemes of the beginning letters of their names. The children will be able to hear different phonemes in words at the beginning, in the middle and at the end. Frequent opportunities for playing with phonemes build the child's confidence in hearing and sounding letters and words in an enjoyable and non-threatening way. For example, an educator noted that Michael had recognised the sound 'm' in Mollie's name. The next day Michael noticed all the class's name cards, which were detachable from a wall display, and took the cards for his friends Andrew and Jack to the educator.

Some of the ideas of using core stories (see Chapter 11) can be applied to using songs for developing knowledge of letters and phonemes in a way that makes sense to children, as well as consolidating their enjoyment of rhyme and rhythm. Core songs and rhymes provide the repetition and reinforcement needed in a way that is enjoyable for the children. Table 12.2 suggests some possibilities.

Singing songs and chanting rhymes can be initiated spontaneously during independent play and learning. The more educators are confident in modelling songs and rhymes, the more children will initiate their own ideas. Changing the words of well known songs and rhymes is another strategy for supporting children's growing knowledge of graphemes and phonemes.

The traditional nursery rhyme *Here We Go Round The Mulberry Bush*[7] lends itself to easy adaptation.

> Here we go round the mulberry bush, the mulberry bush, the mulberry bush,
> Here we go round the mulberry bush, on a cold and frosty morning.
> This is the way we brush our teeth, brush our teeth, brush our teeth,
> This is the way we brush our teeth, on a cold and frosty morning.

Adaptations can include:

> This is the way we build a castle, build a castle, build a castle,
> This is the way we build a castle, when we play and learn.

This focusses on the grapheme 'c' and phoneme /k/.

> This is the way we tidy up, tidy up, tidy up,
> This is the way we tidy up, when we come to school.

This focusses on 't' /t/ and 'u' /u/.

> This is the way we paint a picture, paint a picture, paint a picture,
> This is the way we paint a picture, when we play and learn.

This focusses on 'p' and /p/.

---

6   Website: www.bookstart.org.uk.

7   Harrop B (2001) Here we go round the mulberry bush. In *Sing Hey Diddle Diddle*. A&C Black, London, UK.

## Table 12.1: Graphemes, phonemes and examples[8]

| Graphemes | Phonemes | Examples | Graphemes | Phonemes | Examples | Graphemes | Phonemes | Examples | Graphemes | Phonemes | Examples | Graphemes | Phonemes | Examples |
|---|---|---|---|---|---|---|---|---|---|---|---|---|---|---|
| a | /æ/ | cat | ar | /ɑː/ | art | b | /b/ | but | c | /k/ | call | d | /d/ | do |
| a-e | /eɪ/ | name | au | /ɔː/ | caught | | | | ch | /tʃ/ | church | h | /h/ | house |
| ai | /eɪ/ | pain | aw | /ɔː/ | law | | | | ck | /k/ | back | | | |
| air | /eə/ | pair | ay | /aɪ/ | pay | | | | | | | | | |
| e | /ɛ/ | bed | er | /ɜː/ & /ə/ | her | f | /f/ | fire | g | /g/ | gate | | | |
| e-e | | | ew | /uː/ | few | ff | /f/f/ | cliff | g | /dʒ/ | badge | | | |
| ee | /iː/ | leek | | | | | | | | | | | | |
| ea | /ɛ/ & /iː/ | ear | | | | j | /dʒ/ | joke | k | /k/ | kill | | | |
| i | /ɪ/ | sit | ir | /ɜː/ | girl | | | | | | | l | /l/ | look |
| i-e | /aɪ/ | line | | | | | | | | | | l | /l/ | bill |
| ie | /aɪ/ & /i/ | tied | igh | /aɪ/ | light | | | | or | /ɔː/ | fork | | | |
| m | /m/ | mine | | | | o | /ɒ/ & /əʊ/ | dog | | | | | | |
| | | | n | /n/ | now | oa | /əʊ/ | goat | ou | /aʊ/ & /uː/ & /ʌ/ & /əʊ/ | loud | | | |
| | | | ng | /ŋ/ | going | o-e | /əʊ/ | phone | ow | /aʊ/ & /əʊ/ | owl | | | |
| p | /p/ | play | | | | oi | /ɔɪ/ | oil | oy | /ɔɪ/ | boy | | | |
| ph | /f/ | phone | | | | oo | /uː/ & /ʊ/ | food | s | /s/ & /z/ | stop | t | /t/ | town |
| | | | qu | /k/w/ | queen | r | /r/ | ring | sh | /ʃ/ | shop | th | /θ/ & /ð/ | thing |
| u | /ʌ/ or /ʊ/ & /j/ /uː/ | run | ur | /ɜː/ | fur | v | /v/ | view | ss | /s/ | kiss | | | |
| u-e | /uː/ & /j/ /uː/ | flute | z | /z/ | zip | | | | w | /w/ | went | x | /k/ /s/ | mix |
| y | /j/ | yet | zz | /z/ | fizz | | | | | | | | | |

8   Adapted from phonics screening test framework for pilot. The shaded areas suggest what might be taught first.

# TEACHING LETTERS AND PHONEMES

Table 12.2: Suggestions for letters and phonemes linked to songs

| Graphemes | Phonemes[9] | Song/rhyme | Additions to the continuous provision |
|---|---|---|---|
| r<br>b<br>eam | /r/<br>/b/<br>/ee/ /m/ | *Row, Row, Row Your Boat*[10]<br>Row, row, row your boat<br>Gently down the stream<br>Merrily, merrily, merrily, merrily<br>Life is but a dream | Initiate singing this song when children are playing in the water area.<br><br>Provide different types of boats and materials for children to construct their own boats.<br><br>In music and movement sessions, children sing the song with a partner, gently rocking to the rhythm of the song. |
| d<br><br><br>[s]aid<br><br>at | /d/<br><br><br>/s/ /e/ /d/<br><br>/a/ /t/ | *Dingle Dangle Scarecrow*[11]<br>When all the cows are sleeping and the sun has gone to bed<br>Up jumped the scarecrow and this is what he said<br>I'm a dingle dangle scarecrow with a flippy floppy hat<br>I can shake my hands like this<br>I can shake my feet like that | Farm buildings and farm animals are a focus in the small world area, further enhanced with story and non-fiction books.<br><br>Provide materials outside for creating scarecrows<br><br>Visit a local farm to see animals and scarecrows. |
| h<br>d<br>all | /h/<br>/d/<br>/aw/ /l/ | *Humpty Dumpty*[12]<br>Humpty Dumpty sat on a wall<br>Humpty Dumpty had a great fall<br>All the king's horses and all the king's men<br>Couldn't put Humpty together again | Use a Humpty Dumpty prop to tell the rhyme.<br><br>Role play this traditional nursery rhyme inside and outside.<br><br>Put Humpty Dumpty back together again using a game on Education City[13].<br><br>Build walls in the construction and modelling workshop areas. |
| ss<br>l | /s/<br>/l/ | *There Was a Princess Long Ago*[14]<br>There was a princess long ago, long ago, long ago<br>There was a princess long ago, long long ago<br>And she lived in a big high tower ...<br>One day a bad queen cast a spell ...<br>The princess slept for a hundred years ...<br>A great big forest grew around ...<br>A gallant prince came riding by ...<br>He cut the trees down with his sword ...<br>He took her hand to wake her up ...<br>So everybody's happy now ... | In the art area provide a book illustrating the song using pictures by different artists to motivate the children's own artwork.<br><br>Castle role play with princess, queen and prince costumes and props. |

---

9   Simplified notation.

10  Gadsby D, Harrop B (1982) Row, row, row your boat. *In Flying a Round: 88 rounds and partner songs*. A&C Black, London, UK.

11  *Children's Nursery Favourites. Dingle dangle scarecrow: 26 well loved songs* [audio CD]. CRS Records.

12  Harrop B (2001) Humpty Dumpty. In *Sing Hey Diddle Diddle*. A&C Black, London, UK.

13  Website: www.EducationCity.com (elearning Resources, UK).

14  Gadsby D, Harrop B (2007) There was a princess long ago. In *Apusskidu*. A&C Black, London, UK.

Young children who have had a wealth of experiences to nourish a love of songs and stories, and know that books are a good source of information about their world, naturally reach a point where they are keen to learn how to decode. In other words they are intrinsically motivated to learn about letters and phonemes. To capture this motivation and enthusiasm, the use of whole story and non-fiction texts is more successful than focussing on phonemes in isolation. An important task for educators is to identify stories and non-fiction texts that support the teaching of all the phonemes identified in Table 12.1. Book characters can be a good source. For example, Bob the Builder[15], Max[16] the son of flying superheroes, Meg the witch[17] and Spot the dog[18] are names that children can decode, and use in their own writing, soon having a feeling of success in their literacy learning. With an expanding knowledge and understanding of letters and phonemes, children can blend and read more complex character names, such as Dora the Explorer[19], or Kipper the dog[20].

It is important to ensure these popular texts are always available in the book area. Children can access these texts independently and benefit from constant reinforcement through revisiting. Any books they make themselves based on these characters should also be available to read.

## Texts for phun, and fonics!

### William's Dragons[21]

Stories based on journeys are popular in children's fiction, from traditional tales such as *Chicken Licken*[22] to *We're Going on a Bear Hunt*[23].

In *William's Dragons* a young boy walks through his garden to the woods where he sees a lizard transform into a dragon. The dragon takes him on a journey that leads him to a cave where he discovers a creature called a Glump. Leaving the cave, the boy climbs a high mountain where he uses his red scarf as a flag. Tumbling down the mountain he returns to his garden to the spot where he had seen the lizard.

The story is minimal in text and the illustrations take the children on a fantasy journey. Having shared the story the educator can focus on the name of the creature discovered in the cave, the Glump. Using their knowledge of phonemes, the children can sound out the word and then invent their own names for the different creatures illustrated in the story. This is a starting point for the children to draw, paint, use collage and model their own creatures that live in mysterious caves. The children apply their phonic knowledge in an inventive and creative way.

### Meg on the Moon[24]

The long series of Meg and Mog books provides simple yet interesting texts for children to read. Text is presented in a narrative form as well as in speech bubbles that are part of the illustrations.

An effective way to introduce the Meg stories is to have a set of props for the three main characters, Meg, Mog and Owl. These can be provided in the book area for the children to re-enact the stories and to create their own stories. *Meg on the Moon* can then be used initially to introduce the phoneme /m/. Later it can be used to focus on other phonemes, for example /oo/, as in aaaatishoo,

---

15  HIT Entertainment Ltd (2009) *Bob the Builder*. HIT Entertainment Ltd, London, UK.

16  Graham B (2000) *Max*. Walker Books, London, UK.

17  Nicoll H, Pienkowski J (1976) *Meg on the Moon*. Puffin Books, London, UK.

18  Hill E (1994) *Where's Spot?* Puffin Books, London, UK.

19  Nickelodeon (2010) *Dora's 10 Best Adventures*. Simon and Schuster Children's Books, London, UK.

20  Inkpen M (1999) *Kipper: Story collection*. Hodder Children's Books, London, UK.

21  Baker A (2006) *William's Dragons*. Meadowside Children's Books, London, UK.

22  Ladybird (2008) *Chicken Licken*. Ladybird Books, London, UK.

23  Rosen M (1997) *We're Going on a Bear Hunt*. Walker Books, London, UK.

24  Nicoll, H. and Pienkowski, J. (1973) *Meg on the Moon*. London. Puffin Books, Penguin Group.

# TEACHING LETTERS AND PHONEMES

moon, soon and boom and /oo/ as in oops, look, footprints and took. Words that are onomatopoeic are great to reinforce in children's play, such as /sp/ and /sh/ in splash and /w/ and /ee/ in whee. Playing in puddles provides an ideal opportunity to focus on the word 'splash' and going down the slide fast is a natural reinforcement of whee.

When reading the story *Meg on the Moon* to a group of children, the focus can be either on the characters' names or the words in speech bubbles. These focus words can be provided in the writing area to reinforce and promote application. The following witch's spell:

> Three chunks of cheese,
> A very loud sneeze,
> Man on the moon,
> We'll see you soon.

offers an opportunity for the children to decode a complete text and then to be motivated to create their own spells.

## Aliens Love Underpants[25]

*Aliens Love Underpants* is a text written in rhyme. In addition to their intrinsic value, stories that rhyme support the children's growing awareness of phonemes. Having read the story through several times, the children will enjoy the rhyming words, words that help them to memorise the text and enrich their spoken vocabulary. This is a great text for reinforcing /u/. In the phonic session the children apply their phonic knowledge when sounding out /u/ /n/ /d/ /u/ /p/ /a/ /n/ /t/ /s/. They can show the educator the number of times the word 'underpants' appears in the story. The children can decide which is their favourite part of the story, which is the funniest part of the story and share their ideas for a new story. To follow up the phonic session the children can design their own underpants!

## Walking Through the Jungle[26]

This text presents a song, which, if the educator does not know the tune, can be chanted instead (the song is available in *Game-songs with Prof Dogg's Troupe*)[27]. It offers the opportunity to support the phonic teaching of, for example, /w/ for walking, /th/ for through, /j/ for jungle and /ch/ for chasing. Travelling words like these can be successfully developed both outdoors and in physical education sessions. The educator invites the children to travel around in a way that begins with /w/ and then in a way that begins with /ch/. This idea can be further developed by taking on the children's ideas. They might suggest /j/ for jumping or /s/ for sliding or /h/ for hopping.

## Non-fiction texts to inspire more learning about phonics

### The Happy Little Yellow Box[28]

This is a short text that focusses on positional language, for example 'outside and inside', 'high and low' and 'up and down'. The happy little yellow box features on each page and there are tabs to move and flaps to lift. It can be used to focus on either specific phonemes, such as /h/, /l/, /y/, /b/, or /ks/ as in box. Children love to play with boxes and so there is a lot of potential to develop children's reading skills by providing written suggestions in a box modelling area. Children can make either their own happy little yellow boxes or their own variations.

### Emergency![29]

Young children frequently engage in emergency services role play. This text embraces their enthusiasm. Each page depicts a different emergency service coming to the rescue. The repeated phrase "Help is coming – it's on the way!" is one

25  Freedman C, Cort B (2007) *Aliens Love Underpants*. Simon and Schuster, London, UK.

26  Harter D (1997) *Walking Through the Jungle*. Barefoot Books, Bristol, UK.

27  Powell H (2001) *Game-songs with Prof Dogg's Troupe* [book and audio CD]. Second Edition. A&C Black, London, UK.

28  Carter D A (2010) *The Happy Little Yellow Box. A pop-up book of opposites*. Tango Books Ltd, London, UK.

29  Mayo M, Ayliffe A (2002) *Emergency!* Orchard Books, London, UK.

that can be used to focus on the grapheme and phoneme 'h' /h/. 'Help' can be sounded out and with prompts provided in the writing area can support children's message writing.

## Ask Me[30]

This text presents children with endless questions, the type of questions many children will ask, such as:

● Who is your best friend?

● What would you change if you were the queen or the king?

● What makes you laugh?

● Are you scared of any animals?

Over a week the educator can select different questions to focus on and emphasise the different question words, 'who?', 'which?', 'what?', 'where?', 'whose?' and 'how?' There are also several 'have you ever?' questions. This is a text to facilitate the children's knowledge and understanding of question words and particularly those beginning with the phoneme /w/.

An effective strategy for contextualising phonics learning and teaching is to create stories around puppet characters that reinforce specific phonemes. It is then possible to ensure the focus is not only on the phonemes but is clearly linked to words, sentences and text.

## Where is Fox?
## A week of phonics sessions

The recommendation in the *Letters and Sounds*[31] resource was to plan each phonics session following the format of:

● Revisit and review

● Teach

● Practise

● Apply.

In the following series of sessions the 'teach' element includes the presentation of the whole text, and sometimes a caption or sentence, before breaking it down to specific phonemes. Phonemes are therefore presented within a meaningful context and not in isolation.

Prior to the first session photographs are taken of Fox in different areas of the setting: Fox 'in' her box, 'on' her box, and 'under' her box.

Put together a photo book called *Where is Fox?* with the pages as follows:

1　Where is Fox?
2　Fox is in the box
3　Fox is on the box
4　Fox is under the box.

## Where is Fox? Session one

The children sit in a circle. The 15 minute phonics session starts with an alphabet song. This song reinforces the letter names. The educator introduces Fox and shows the children the photographs of Fox playing in the different areas of provision (photographs can either be presented in a book or on an interactive whiteboard). The photo book is read together then the children sound out /f/ /o/ /ks/. Questions follow: what other words rhyme with fox? The educator demonstrates how to write f o x, and provides small handheld whiteboards for the children to write the word 'fox' themselves.

The phonics session is reinforced in the continuous provision by providing:

● A copy of the *Where is Fox?* book in the book area, writing area and small world play area

---

30　Damm A (2005) *Ask Me*. Frances Lincoln Children's Books, London, UK.

31　Primary National Strategy (2007) *Letters and Sounds: Principles and practice of high quality phonics. Six-phase teaching programme*. Department for Education and Skills, London, UK.

- A fox soft toy in the construction area. Invite the children to build a home for Fox

- Fox figures in the small world area

- Non-fiction texts in the book area about wild animals and habitats

- Copies of the images used in the phonics session in the writing area

- Furry fabrics for children to create their own representations of Fox in the collage and modelling areas.

## Where is Fox? Session two

The session starts with recall of yesterday's phonics session. Fox is brought out to sing an alphabet song with the children. Fox's box and the photo book are shown to the children. The story is read and some words are sounded out. Rhyming words are recalled from yesterday. This time they are listed. The children's attention is drawn to how some of the rhyming words are spelt differently but sound the same. One focus is on /s/ /o/ /ks/, both sounding out and writing. Nonsense rhymes are invented, for example:

> Fox in the box
> Wearing socks!
> Pink socks
> And purple!
> Orange socks
> And blue!

Additions to the continuous provision:

- Different pairs of socks, soapy water and washing lines inside and out

- Prompts for children to design their own 'silly socks'

- Pairs of socks to sort in the home corner

- Socks in the workshop area for children to make sock puppets.

## Where is Fox? Session three

Before the start of the session Fox is placed in an area of provision. The alphabet song is sung again. The children are presented with a dilemma, Fox is lost. Who can find Fox? The children are given some clues using the photographs of Fox in different areas of provision and provided with plans of the setting. Could she be in the home corner? Could she be in the painting area? Two children are asked to search for Fox. On their return the children are encouraged to recall the *Where is Fox?* story, and their *Fox and Socks* rhymes and all the different activities they did with socks. The children write their own *Fox and Socks* rhymes either on handheld whiteboards or clipboards with paper.

Next the children discover a note which has been pinned onto Fox. The note says, "Can you find Goldilocks?" They note that Goldilocks rhymes with 'fox' and 'socks'. The message is read and sounded out with the children. The challenge for the children is to find Goldilocks in their setting.

Additions to the continuous provision:

- Setting maps with different trails marked out for the children to use to find Goldilocks.

- Setting maps for the children to create their own trails.

- Goldilocks story books and props in the different areas of provision for the children to find and collect. Picnic baskets are provided for gathering the props.

## Where is Fox? Session four

The fourth session starts with the song, *When Goldilocks Went to the House of the Bears*[32]. The children are asked, "Did anyone find Goldilocks?" The children's responses are collated. The original text, *Where is Fox?*, the *Fox and Socks* rhyme, and the new rhymes the children have written themselves are revisited. Copies of a selection of the children's rhymes are given out for them to read in talk partners. Questions are asked: What do they like about the rhymes? How could the rhymes be improved? The children revisit the rhymes, writing them out again, or editing the copy they have been given. The rhymes are celebrated with readings.

Additions to the continuous provision:

- Copies of the children's rhymes to illustrate in the writing and art areas

- Design sheets in the construction area to motivate children to design and build the house of the three bears

- The talk machine for the children to perfect their *Fox and Socks* rhyme performances.

## Where is Fox? Session five

The song, *When Goldilocks Went to the House of the Bears* is sung again. The conclusion for this series of phonics sessions is reading the complete text of *Fox in Socks*[33]. This presents the higher attaining children with further challenges as the text becomes increasingly complex.

# Games to support the children's learning of letters and phonemes

## I Spy

The traditional game of I Spy remains one of the best ways to engage children in identifying the beginning phoneme (and/or letter) of words. I Spy can also be developed to include the middle and end phonemes of words. Playing I Spy on a regular basis, and having the props available in the continuous provision, ensures that educators continue to focus on the oral aspects of developing children's application of phonics.

## Rattle, Rattle, Rattle the Box

In Rattle, Rattle, Rattle the Box, either objects, letters or words can be placed in the box and children take it in turns to:

> Rattle, rattle, rattle the box

---

### Box 12.1: Story for Zork the Sorting Robot

One day Zork the sorting robot found a pile of words. She picked them up and counted them, "One, two, three, four!" "What do they say?", she asked herself.

Zork read out, "save", "rocket", "my", "please". "That doesn't make sense", said Zork, "I shall have to find out what the words mean".

Zork put the words in her silver word bag and walked on.

Zork met Bing the eco robot. "Look what I found", Zork said. "Four pieces of card that say, 'save', 'rocket', 'my', 'please'. What can they mean?"

"They're in the wrong order. We need to sort them out!" said Bing.

---

> Rattle, rattle, rattle the box
> How many words can you read?

Words are provided that can be combined to make meaningful sentences. This is another game that children can self-initiate and then practise their phonics with confidence.

## Zork the Sorting Robot

Children sound out Zork the robot's name. The character of Zork is presented in a story (see Box 12.1). The storytelling is supported with cardboard cut-out props to represent each character. The characters are Zork the sorting robot and Bing the eco robot. The children sort the words for Zork into those that are 'or' words and those that are not.

## Lotto

Another traditional game *Lotto* can contribute to children's developing phonic awareness. For example with a picture version the caller says 'this is a picture beginning with.....'

---

32  Harrop B (ed) (1976; current edition 2010) When Goldilocks went to the house of the bears. In *Okki-tokki-unga*. A&C Black, London, UK.

33  Dr Seuss (1965) *Fox in Socks*. Random House, London, UK.

# TEACHING LETTERS AND PHONEMES

and the children predict which picture it is from the picture cards they have. As children gain in confidence the caller has cards with letters, calls out the phoneme and the children find a corresponding picture or word. As children's confidence with phonemes develop they enjoy the idea of alliteration. Identifying a string of words starting with the same phoneme brings in humour for the children.

As well as the planned daily phonics sessions, young children need to be supported in their understanding of the alphabetic code during their independent play and learning. Through observations and the collation of the children's writing, the educator can build up a picture of each child's progress in applying their knowledge of letters and phonemes.

Here is an example of a child's development of letters and phonemes knowledge.

Zakiyah is a multilingual learner in a Foundation Stage/ Reception class:

- 5th January 2011: Zakiyah selects her name label from the wall.

- 24th January 2011: Zakiyah blends the phonemes /j/ /e/ /t/ together to make "jet".

- 14th February 2011: Zakiyah is playing the Zork the Sorting Robot game. I say /h/ /ur/ /t/. She whispers "hurt".

- 21st March 2011: Zakiyah sits on a bench outside. She watches and listens to her friend drawing a girl called "Pat". She writes the name for her friend.

- 4th April 2011: Zakiyah sits at the writing table. She says, "I can write now". She writes "mum". "Look! I can write 'mum'", she says.

- 20th May 2011: Zakiyah writes on the whiteboard "I fl hapee". She writes a series of words, "box", "mum", "cat" and then writes the letters 'x', 'v', 'w', 'y'. All the letters are formed correctly.

- 4th July 2011: Zakiyah writes the instructions for how to make a necklace (see Figure 12.1).

**Figure 12.1: Zakiyah's instructions on how to make a necklace**

Zakiyah has sufficient knowledge of phonemes to blend and segment. She applies these skills to her reading and writing. Zakiyah shows she is excited about her achievement by saying, "Look! I can write 'mum'". Children who are able to articulate their learning strengthen the learning process and the educators are able to evidence the children's progress.

When Zakiyah decides to write the instructions on how to make a necklace she has both the confidence and skills to be successful in this task. Her writing is effectively laid out, it is legible and she has applied her phonic knowledge to spell the majority of words.

This example shows how important it is to keep dated records of children's achievements so that their progress is clear to both educators and parents.

# CHAPTER 13

# Texts for writing

Painting and making marks with a brush and water in a pre-school setting

The issues of breadth and depth are relevant to writing just as they are to reading. Educators need to introduce children to a sufficiently wide range of written texts, but it is important that children also experience opportunities to explore particular types of writing in more depth. In the early stages of writing development children's texts are created opportunistically on resources that come to hand. Pictures and print-like marks are mixed together.

As children develop, they understand the characteristics of different texts. Some of the texts that they should encounter are: lists; diaries and reports (including newspaper style); reviews, such as book reviews; poetry; letters and other forms of communication. Narrative and story writing

are powerful forms for most children. When children are encouraged to write their own stories their creativity can be a delight for educators and a powerful vehicle for motivating children to write. In addition to offering children choice over the kinds of writing they do, at other times educators will use directed activities to stimulate writing. One of the many aspects of writing that children have to develop is their understanding of the ways in which different texts are structured. One of the most commonly cited ideas about story structure is that they have a beginning, middle and end (or as Philip Larkin mischievously suggested a beginning, muddle and end). The genre theorists[1] attempted to develop a set of categories that could apply to all stories (see Box 13.1).

1   Martin J, Christie F, Rothery J (1987) Social processes in education: A reply to Sawayer and Watson (and others). In I Reid (ed) *The Place of Genre in Learning*. Deakin University, Victoria, Australia.

# TEXTS FOR WRITING

At text level, narrative structures like story structures are one way that writing maintains cohesion. Each stage requires the one before it if the text is to make sense. Of course one of the interesting things about any kind of model like this is the way that so many story texts simply do not conform. Helping children understand the key features of different kinds of texts, through analysis of real examples of the genre (not pseudo-examples of genres in published schemes) is another element of teaching writing strategies.

Young children in early years settings are enthusiastic about making their own marks when the materials are readily available within the continuous provision. It is the educator's role to encourage and support all children to access resources, to praise significant features of children's mark-making, and to take children's learning forward through sensitive feedback that nurtures their confidence.

Children are acute observers and the more they see adults writing and reading, the more they want to imitate and have a go for themselves. It is essential that the children have the opportunity to make their marks independently. Educators need to build on their observations of children in order to extend their understanding. This will include a wide range of teaching, but it is not the educator's role to make the marks for the child unless they are scribing their meaning to facilitate written composition. Children's independent mark-making tells us so much about their understanding. When educators work in this way children soon learn that the educators value their writing.

The following observations illustrate texts and contexts that helped to motivate children and develop their writing.

## Faiza – age 5 years

- Faiza has drawn a picture of herself and her house, and has written her own name (see Figure 13.1) and used her knowledge of letters and sounds to write "has" for house and "jup" for jump.

- Faiza is asked to write about her favourite fairy tale (see

| Box 13.1: Story structure | |
|---|---|
| Abstract | The title, *Little Red Riding Hood*, and introductory material: once upon a time ... |
| Orientation | A forest and a journey to grandmother's cottage |
| Complication | Red Riding Hood meets the wolf dressed as her grandmother |
| Evaluation | She runs away and finds the woodcutter |
| Resolution | The woodcutter kills the wolf |
| Coda | The moral – something that was explicitly written as a separate section in the original versions |

Figure 13.2). She writes about Cinderella but also uses her knowledge of the song *The Princess*[2].

- Faiza writes about her family (see Figure 13.3).

- Two months later Faiza retells the story of *Jack and the Beanstalk* (see Figure 13.4).

## Ali – age 6 years

- The children have studied the life of Mary Seacole. Their writing task is to answer the question, "Why is Mary Seacole famous?" (see Figure 13.5).

- Two months later Ali writes a poem about a cat (see Figure 13.6).

- Four months later Ali writes his version of *The Lighthouse Keeper's Lunch*[3] (see Figure 13.7).

---

2  Harrop B (ed) (1976; current edition 2010) The princess. In *Okki-tokki-unga*. A&C Black, London, UK.

3  Armitage D, Armitage R (1994) *The Lighthouse Keeper's Lunch*. Scholastic Hippo, London, UK.

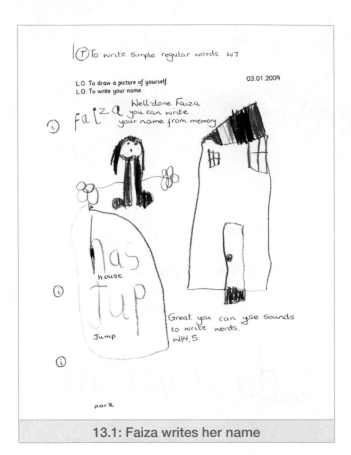

(T) To write simple regular words  W7

L.O. To draw a picture of yourself
L.O. To write your name                    03.01.2009

:)   FAIZA   Well-done Faiza
              you can write
              your name from memory

:)   has
     house
     JUp
     Jump                Great you can yse sounds
                         to write words.
                         W3,4,5
:)

park

**13.1: Faiza writes her name**

FAIZA

Writing about my favourite fairy tale

Sintreter When the Prins comes  I
Like  When  the  Fairree  god Muther
I like  When  the  Prins comes to
cis on her hand  When  the  Fairree god
Muther  cast Peta spel  I like  when
evree budee was happy noww
I Like When all of the Pedal
go to the caisil  I Like When
I Like When evree budee
have a Paitee

**13.2: Faiza writes about her favourite fairy tale**

Writing (1) own version of a familiar story. July 2010
   08.07.2010.   Jacks mum was
DeD Then his PaP Looked at The
Pror Then  his pan said. There isunt
any Food. Then  his pap said Sell
The cow. Then Jack saw a man
Then The man said I will have
This cow. Jack said will you,
have  Then Jack said He whent
to home. Then Jack made it
home. Then He shoad The Beans
to his PaP. Then his PaP Throd
The magic beans out side. Then
Jack Looked out side his
window  he saw  a big bean stalk
Then his PaP said get down
Jack said get down He said
no.

Writing (2) own version of a familiar story. July 2010
Then Jack saw a big Flower.
Then He said wow. Then he saw a
big Tree. There was lots eyes meet eyumd
cars He saw no Pople in The cars Then
He said wow. he saw a big castle He
noced on The castles poor no one
opeled The Poor He squilled
Throu The poor Then He saw a
big giants Table He saw
everey Think  was cold He
saw a goose He saw it sad
The goose said  can I go
with you. The giant saw The
goose and Jack goi wing down
The bean stalk The giant
was clam ing on The beanstalk Jacksag
                              give me The ax.

**13.4: Faiza's own version of the familiar
story of *Jack and the Beanstalk***

# TEXTS FOR WRITING

FIZA

## my famlee

24.05.2010

MUM Gramal

SADA ALLAN FAIZA

Ayesha ALIL

DaD

I Like to helP my mum to helP my mum to whosh the dishis. I like my Dady bikus He talks me to queens park. My Dad Likesto goo to Pakistul). My bruther dysunt Like a cow. My DaD is a taucsee dright ver. my BIg Bruther Likes to Play Busketboll. We got a hous at Pakis.

---

**Figure 13.3: My famlee by Faiza**

10.12. Rob Why is mary seacole Famous?
famous?
In 1805 mary born in kingstoton
Jamaica I In 1805 Mary was born.
mary helPed her mum as mary gloo up
She wanted to be a nurse.
She bravled to other othair
kuntrees. She heard that the soldier's wele
dieng She thwent went and help the soldier's.
She w went and ask the men in charchchargj
the men in charch charj said no.
The men were Fighting. The soldier's swele
not only been wounded called cholera.
The soldier's wele really hungry
mary put in a bag food medisun and drink.
evryday the soldier's wul cannul mary.
In 1856 mary had no money.
She wirwisrted about her adv adventure's.
mary died In 1881. Mary as being a brave
nurse. Mary is Famous being a brave nurse becuase
She helped the soldier's.

---

**13.5: Ali's answer to the question: "Why is Mary Seacole famous?"**

17.02.2011

I came across a cat.
On the way to School.
It had sharp teeth and clors.
The cat had bright eyes.
The cat was so stripy.
It was so Soft.
The cat had strip Stripy wiskers.
it had blue eyes.
The cat was so fury.
The cat is brown.
The cat's was noise is pink.
It is play full.
it is has a long tail.
it is smooth.
The cat has a mouth.
I took the cat home.

---

**13.6: Ali's cat poem**

18.07.2011 Monday 18 July 2011

Once upon there was little white coalage perched on a hard cliff. One Monday morning she made an appetising lunch she made an appetising bread and some delicious delitous lunch. She cliped it on to the wire and send it of to the Lighthouse. But three scavenging seaguls ate the lunch and Mr grinling sail. go away
On Tusday Mrs Grinling con cooking Mr grinlings lunch. Unfourtunatly the thice scavenging seaguls came. On Wenesday she put Hamish the cat in the basket. And she cliped it onto the wire and send it off to the Lighthouse. But the three scavenging seaguls still ate the lunch. On Thursday she had an ingenious plan she put mustard sandwiche's in the bread. Then she send it off to the Lighthouse. After that the seaguls came and they said yuk. On Friday she mad an scrumptious lunch and Mr grinling was full.

---

**Figure 13.7: Ali's version of**
***The Lighthouse Keeper's Lunch***

# CHAPTER 14

# The learning environment for writing

Writing area display

Although reading can be supported simply by a good selection of books and other texts, the resources required for writing are more numerous. The most basic selection is of course paper and pencils or pens. But even thinking about paper alone raises a series of issues. Exercise books are useful as a way to keep children's writing together in sequence, but paper, both lined and unlined, has the advantage that it can be used to display writing on walls and in books made in the classroom. Paper can also be thrown away when the writer is not content with the writing. Perhaps still the most under-used tool in early years and primary settings is the computer which can be used for drafting and writing from first draft. Children

should have frequent opportunities to start their first draft using a computer. Once children are familiar with computer hardware and software redrafting can be so much easier than on hard copy. Computers also allow for a much wider range of text production, ranging from the simple inclusion of illustrations with children's writing, through to multi-media work including moving images and sound.

In early years settings at least one designated writing area can be a powerful way to entice children to write, draw and mark-make. Ideally the area should be organised so that children have easy access to a range of resources which they

# THE LEARNING ENVIRONMENT FOR WRITING

can help themselves to. It should also be organised to allow for children to easily be able to tidy up. Comfortable tables or desks to write on are essential. If space allows, then children may also like to lie out on the floor to write. Permanent resources in the writing area should include:

- Writing implements, such as felt pens and other things for colouring

- A range of papers, including lined, unlined, different coloured papers and card, if possible

- Book-making equipment such as staplers and comb-binding machines

- A range of pre-constructed blank booklets

- Reporters' pads.

Some special, more expensive resources can also be occasionally introduced. Writing can also be encouraged in other areas of the learning environment and even outside, but these opportunities should be purposeful.

Displays of writing, particularly children's writing, are important, as is text that can help children when they are writing, such as alphabet friezes, reminders of strategies to help with writing, key words, words of the week and posters. Research shows that print-rich learning environments lead to gains in literacy development[1].

Writing areas are also labelled as mark-making areas in early years settings. It is important for young children that they do not experience early failure as young writers. The term 'mark-making' values those initial marks children make on paper. For the child the marks may either be an initial exploration of materials, or marks that are a visual representation, or marks that represent the printed word. Young children will describe their marks and will identify what is a picture and what is writing. This again highlights the value of interaction between child and adult. Writing areas need to capture the child's intrinsic motivation to make marks, to write and to engage in book-making. The following two sections provide ideas for

the provision of a writing area for three year olds and a book-making area for six year olds.

## Resources for three year olds

Basic provision ought to include:

- Pencils

- Coloured pencils

- Marker pens

- Felt pens

- Biros

- Paper of different sizes, shapes and colours

- Different types of paper, including lined and squared

- Collection of notepads

- Post-it notes

- Clipboards

- Stapler and staples

- Hole punch and stationery tags

- Paper clips.

## Resources for six year olds

By the age of six, children need to be able to make books independently. These include books that are:

- Folded, including zigzag books

- Stapled

---

1   Sailors M, Hoffman J (2010) The text environment and learning to read: Windows and mirrors shaping literate lives. In D Wyse, R Andrews, J Hoffman (eds) *The Routledge International Handbook of English, Language and Literacy Teaching*. Routledge, London, UK.

**Book-making area for six year olds**

**A three year old accesses the mark-making area**

- Sewn

- Ready-made blank books for children to either draw and write in or stick their work in.

An inspiring book-making area will have all the basics of a writing area as described in the previous section, plus:

- Instructions to show how to make different types of books, including pop-up books

- Photographs, ordered in sequence, to visually show how to make different types of books

- Labels and prompts to motivate children to access the book-making area

- A display showcasing books that have been made by the children

- Sample books

- Access to a computer for typing up books and including photographs

- Non-fiction books that illustrate the book-making process.

Another source of meaningful texts to share with children is those created by educators themselves. This would occur when the educators want to inspire children who are reluctant to engage in texts. Photobooks are easy to make and are proven to be successful. The development from self-made books is for children to engage in their own book-making. Although IT publishing may not be available to all educators, it is becoming increasingly so.

The observations shown in Figures 14.1 and 14.2 recorded what children did when they accessed the writing and book-making areas.

# THE LEARNING ENVIRONMENT FOR WRITING

Figure 14.1: Child observation in an early years setting: three year old writing in the writing area

| | |
|---|---|
| **Child's name:** Lily | **Child's age:** 3 years 9 months |
| **Date of observation:** 6th October 2011 | **Length of observation:** 5 minutes |
| **Location:** Writing area | **Keyworker:** Catherine |

**Description**

Lily decides to go to the writing area and she selects a small whiteboard and black pen. She sits at the table and is soon making marks. Lily holds the pen in her left hand and makes marks with confidence. She uses a paper towel to wipe out her marks. Lily draws a horizontal mark from left to right. Lily shows high levels of involvement and is not distracted by anything going on around her.

**Note:** Photograph taken

**Reflections**

Lily is very content to be engaged in activities on her own. Does Lily mark-make in other areas of provision? Does she show an interested in the printed word, either in the book area or in the environment?

**Next steps**

- Continue to observe Lily in her self-chosen activities.

- Note if she is playing alongside other children.

- Note if she repeats horizontal lines, or combines with vertical lines.

**Parent/s comment/s**

Lily's big sister: Lily's just started to say she wants to draw pictures. We've bought her some new felt pens and she draws and draws; nothing disturbs her!

**Figure 14.2: Child observation in an early years setting: six year old writing in the book-making area**

| | |
|---|---|
| **Child's name:** Haidar | **Child's age:** 6 years 5 months |
| **Date of observation:** 10th October 2011 | **Length of observation:** 5 minutes |
| **Location:** Book-making area | **Keyworker:** Amanda |

**Description**

We have just enhanced our book-making provision by providing visual instructions on how to make a pop-up book. The instructions are in sequenced photographs. Haidar immediately decided to make his own pop-up book. He positioned the photographs directly in front of himself and carefully followed the instructions. Haidar selected a piece of paper and folded it in half. He drew two lines ready to cut. Haidar made a small fold and then by unfolding the paper created his pop-up.

**Note:** Photograph taken

**Reflections**

Haidar can follow the pop-up book instructions and demonstrates confident paper-folding and cutting skills.

**Next steps**

- Plan for children to have time to make their own pop-up books.

- Provide time for them to plan the book, the text and the illustrations and then to put the book together. Theme? Self-chosen or based on the current class theme?

**Parent/s comment/s**

Haidar's mother: I was surprised to see Haidar could follow these instructions. I am going to look for a book about pop-ups for home. Maybe I can find something on the internet.

CHAPTER 15 ......

# Strategies for writing

**Alishba chooses to write about her favourite clothes she wears at weddings**

One of the key issues when planning the teaching of writing is what kind of stimulus to offer. In other words, the educator has to decide what kind of encouragement, activities and experiences children need in order to help them to write. These decisions should be affected by consideration of children's motivation. Most teachers make the sensible assumption that when children are not motivated, they do not learn as well as they could (see Chapter 2).

When planning the kind of activities to stimulate children's writing, it is helpful to think of a continuum between loosely-structured and tightly-structured approaches. Tightly-structured approaches very clearly prescribe the kind of texts or extracts of texts that children are expected to produce. Loosely-structured approaches give children much more opportunity to make choices over their writing. As an example of a loosely-structured approach, the 'process approach' has an enviable track record in motivating children to write and is based on establishing authorship in the classroom supported by a publishing process[1].

The most important feature of the process approach to teaching writing is that children are offered choice over what to write. This is not just choice within a genre prescribed by the educator, but real choice over the topic and type of writing. One of the classic techniques is to ask children to generate a list of five things that they would like to write, then to choose one and get writing.

---

1   Wyse D (1998) *Primary Writing*. Open University Press, Buckingham, UK.

......

The key elements of the process approach are:

- Regular writing workshops

- A publishing cycle in the classroom

- Writing seen as a process that requires drafting and redrafting

- Extended opportunities for writing to completion

- Writing with real audiences in mind

- Mini-lessons to work on writing skills and understanding

- One-to-one interaction with the educator to support writing.

The texts that are a core focus for reading can also be used to stimulate writing. Thinking about different versions, sequels and taking the characters into a new context are all examples of ways to use high quality texts as a stimulus. Drama and role play are also used to stimulate writing, sometimes linked to a core text or simply as a way of generating ideas.

The use of artefacts and first-hand experiences can lead to writing that is either loosely-structured or tightly-structured. Artefacts and other physical resources are a well-established means of stimulating writing through a creative writing approach.

Writing frames are another popular way of supporting children in their writing, particularly non-fiction writing[2]. Writing frames are guides to different forms of writing that include possible sentence starts and reminders about things to include. However, educators must always remember that not all children benefit from writing frames, and the goal is to encourage children's independence to write without such frameworks.

Children need to be taught strategies that will help their writing. For example, learning to summarise texts that have been read helps writing because it can be used as a way to illustrate that writing requires conciseness and accuracy. Other strategies children need to be taught include:

- Planning writing

- Revising

- Editing

- Structural ideas such as headings and paragraphs.

Teaching writing strategies is helped by the educator modelling the writing using a flipchart or board (interactive or traditional), and interacting with children on a one-to-one basis to discuss their writing and help them improve it. For children in the earliest stages educators can also act as scribes for children's ideas.

## Four year olds

### Strategies for story writing

When children's mark-making is valued by educators they naturally ask for their stories to be scribed. These can be handwritten as well as presented in printed form.

Farid told his version of the traditional tale *The Three Billy Goats Gruff*, which the educator scribed for him.

> The Billy Goats went to the bridge and the troll said, "No you can't" and the three Billy Goats chucked him in the water. The Billy Goats went up to the bridge and they went, "Hooray!"

Alia combined her knowledge of stories, popular culture, and familiar adults.

> Miss Porter is a princess. Then a big dragon put her in a dark, dark cave. Then the princess said, "Open the light". Then the dragon said, "No, because you are scared of me". Then the mother and father said "Can you rescue the princess?" Then the king said, "Yes I will". Then he go to the bridge and go slowly and slowly then he go faster because the rope was going down. Then he go in the king's house and he said "Have you got the light sabre to help the princess?" Then the dragon be good.

---

2   Wray D, Lewis M (1997) *Extending Literacy: Children reading and writing non-fiction*. Routledge, London, UK.

# STRATEGIES FOR WRITING

**Figure 15.1: Lucy's rainbow puppet**

**Figure 15.2: Subhan's writing about owls**

Educators also scribe while children are engaged in learning in the different areas of continuous provision. Here is an example.

Lucy, four years old, had made a rainbow puppet (see Figure 15.1) by drawing a rainbow on a semicircular piece of paper and attaching it to a lollipop stick. This inspired her to make up her own rainbow song, which the educator scribed:

> The rainbow, the rainbow
> Lucy makes a rainbow all by herself
> Pink and yellow and purple and blue
> Red and purple and blue!

Scribing children's spoken words while they are engaged in a range of activities develops their awareness of writing, especially if they do not readily choose to work in the writing area.

When children's writing is published, for example in book form or electronic form, the children are then able to illustrate the text. The children create texts for other children as the 'audience' to read, and this further motivates them to create more stories and accounts. The process of revisiting drafts of writing as books are made provides a natural opportunity for redrafting and learning more about conventional forms of printed language.

## Six year olds

## First-hand experience as a stimulus

First-hand experiences inspire children to write.

The following example illustrates the success of a visit by a bird sanctuary's member of staff with their birds to the class.

The core story for the Year 2 class of multilingual children was *The Owl Who Was Afraid of the Dark*[3]. The educators knew that the children would benefit from seeing a real owl because most wouldn't have seen one before.

Figure 15.3: A information map about owls

## Writing about owls – session one

The educator explained to the class that they were to have a visit from the bird sanctuary, and that the purpose of this visit was to support them in their writing about owls (see Figure 15.2), which would be reproduced in a book format for everyone to take home.

In their talk partners the children discussed what that might mean. Having established that their visitor would be bringing some owls for them to observe, the children discussed possible questions for their visitor.

The educator collated their questions on a flipchart and throughout the school day revisited the list so that the children had the opportunity to add to it.

The children were now looking forward to the visit and many were keen to tell their parents and carers.

## Writing about owls – session two

In the school hall the children experienced seeing the four owls brought by the visitor from the bird sanctuary. One educator took photographs to capture this shared experience and to consolidate new vocabulary. While the children observed, the visitor provided information about the owls as well as answering the children's pre-prepared questions. The educators prompted accuracy and clarity. One educator scribed the dialogue.

## Writing about owls – session three

The third session followed immediately after the visit. Images of the visit were projected onto the interactive whiteboard and working with a writing partner the children were asked to create an information map of their knowledge and understanding of owls. An information map provides a format for the children to record all that they know about

3   Tomlinson J (2004) *The Owl Who Was Afraid of the Dark*. Egmont Books Ltd, London, UK.

# STRATEGIES FOR WRITING

Figure 15.4: A story map for *Jack and the Beanstalk*

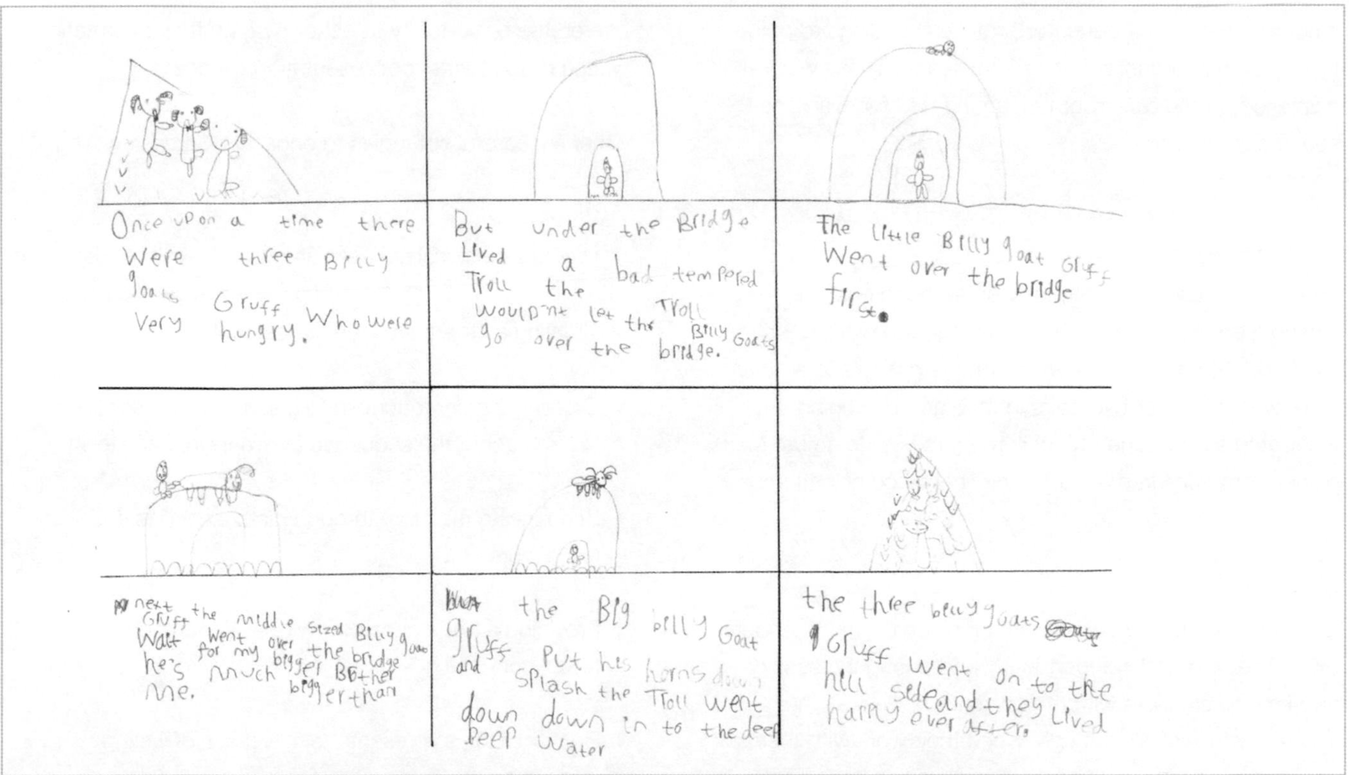

Figure 15.5: A story sequence for *The Three Billy Goats Gruff*

**Figure 15.6: Zulaika writes a speech bubble for one of the Billy Goats Gruff**

**Figure 15.7: Zara's book telling the story of** *The Three Billy Goats Gruff*

a specific topic. The educator provides headings to guide the children in organising their knowledge. These were all displayed on the classroom's learning wall for everyone to see and to refer to.

## Writing about owls – session four

The children used their information maps to plan their writing (see Figure 15.3). They continued to work in writing partners. When the plans were complete they shared their work with the other two pairs in their group. Finding out what others had done, the children had time to adjust their plans. Some children started their final piece of writing.

## Writing about owls – session five

Children had time to complete their piece of writing about owls. They worked independently and during the session had time to check in with their writing partner. As they finished their writing, they swapped their work with their writing partners to mark each others' writing in colour to show any grammatical and punctuation errors. They were

offered the opportunity to either type up their information writing or to rewrite for presentation purposes.

Other successful strategies to engage children in writing include:

● Drawing a pictorial representation before writing a description

● Creating a story map (see Figure 15.4)

● Creating a story mountain to encourage the children to think about the sequence of events in their story

● Sequencing the story through pictures and text (see Figure 15.5)

● Providing a book character with a speech bubble (see Figure 15.6)

● Book-making to present the final piece of writing (see Figure 15.7).

# CHAPTER 16

# Grammar and punctuation

Role play and drama can be used to explore different levels of formality within language

Grammar is a feature of any language that enables meanings to be expressed. From the point of view of prescriptive grammarians, the grammar of the standard dialect known as Standard English is 'good' or 'correct' grammar, and the grammar of non-standard dialects is 'bad' or 'incorrect' grammar. So, for example, children who say "I ain't done nothing" often have their language 'corrected' by their educators, and even by their own parents, on the ground that it is 'bad' grammar, or indeed, more generally, that it is just 'bad' English.

Descriptive grammarians are interested in describing how the language actually is used rather than how it ought to be used. A descriptive grammarian will note that a middle-class speaker, using Standard English, may say: "We were pleased to see you", and that a working-class speaker using a working-class Cockney dialect may say: "We was pleased to see you". Both examples are grammatical within their own dialects, both examples make perfect sense, and in neither example is there any ambiguity. The idea that a plural subject takes a plural verb is true only of the middle-class standard dialect, not of the working-class Cockney dialect. To put it another way, the plural form of the verb in middle-class standard is 'were', while the plural form of the verb in working-class Cockney is 'was'.

Some of the controversy about grammar is a confusion between use of language and technical descriptions of language or grammar (something called metalanguage or language to describe language). For example, the definitions 'a noun is a naming word', 'a verb is a doing word' are at best unhelpful and at worst downright misleading. Though meaning has a part to play in determining the relationship between words, parts of speech are not defined in terms of word meaning, they are defined, rather, in terms of the function of the words within the sentence. As an example of what we mean, think about the word 'present'.

Present can be a verb:

> I present you with this tennis racket as a reward for your services.

or a noun:

> Thank you for my birthday present. I've always wanted socks!

or an adjective:

> In the present circumstances I feel unable to proceed.

It is clear, then, that teaching grammar has its problems. Confusion can occur at a number of levels: between prescriptive and descriptive approaches, between questions of grammar proper and questions of style, and around issues of variation between standard and non-standard dialects.

The teaching of reading and writing, of spelling and punctuation, requires the continual use of metalanguage such as: alphabet; letter; word; spelling; sentence; and full stop.

In addition, many educators take the opportunities offered by reading and writing to draw children's attention to specific items of vocabulary. Much of this specific attention to language itself is at the word and sentence level.

Research has clearly shown that formal decontextualised grammar teaching does not have a positive effect on children's writing[1]. However, children do need to learn how to control grammar as one of the various essential aspects of writing. The most effective way to focus on improvements in grammar is through editing and redrafting of writing. A very good starting point when working with children is the question "Can you think how to improve that?", or "Could you write that a

different way?" If, after encouragement through these kinds of questions, a child cannot see how to improve writing, then the educator will of course offer suggestions. An important feature of written language is how sentences and phrases of different length are combined to create meaning in ways that achieve particular effects related to the genre of writing. One way that this can be investigated is through exploring how sentences and phrases can be combined to change meaning.

In addition to the value of close textual editing, more generally the starting point for work on grammar is encouraging children to discuss language use in meaningful contexts that engage their interest. Here are some examples of work done in primary schools[2]:

- Making word lists.

- Compiling dictionaries, including slang and dialect dictionaries.

- Discussing language variation and social context. For example, how does a mobile phone text message compare with a formal letter?

- Discussing accent, and Standard English.

- Compiling personal language histories and language profiles.

- Capitalising on the language resource of the multilingual classroom beginning with in-depth knowledge of languages spoken, read, written and their social contexts including religious ones.

- Role play and drama, particularly to explore levels of formality and their links with language.

- The history and use of language in the local environment.

- Collecting and writing jokes.

---

1   Wyse D (2001) Grammar for writing? A critical review of empirical evidence. *British Journal of Educational Studies*, 49 (4), 411-427.

  Andrews R, Torgerson C, Beverton S, Locke T, Low G, Robinson A, Zhu D (2004) The effect of grammar teaching (syntax) in English on 5 to 16 year olds' accuracy and quality in written composition. EPPI-Centre Evidence Library (available from http://eppi.ioe.ac.uk/cms/).

2   Bain R, Fitzgerald B, Taylor M (1992) *Looking into Language: Classroom approaches to knowledge about language*. Hodder & Stoughton, Sevenoaks, UK.

# GRAMMAR AND PUNCTUATION

- Collaborative writing which involves discussion about features of writing and language.

- Media work including the language of advertising.

- Book-making.

Many of the examples in this list could be, and indeed were, done with the youngest children, and terminology was learned in context as and when the children needed it in their work.

Punctuation is no different from writing in general in that the generation of meaning is the primary function of written language: punctuation is learned most successfully in the context of rich and meaningful writing experiences[3].

In the early stages children use non-linguistic punctuation rather than linguistic punctuation[4]. An example of non-linguistic punctuation is where a child puts full stops at the end of every line of a piece of writing rather than at the end of the sentences. This illustrates the child's belief that punctuation is to do with position and space rather than to indicate meaning and structure. It is important that educators focus on explanation of punctuation, including the differences between punctuation marks, rather than focus on naming and procedures. For example take the procedure: always put a full stop at the end of a sentence. The problem with this is that you have to know what a sentence is in order to know where to put the full stop. This does not require technical definitions that rely on grammatical knowledge about clauses, but it does require children to compare text fragments and discuss whether they are sentences or not.

One somewhat ephemeral but useful idea is that a sentence feels complete. This means that a sentence makes complete sense on its own. This is not the same as saying a sentence always ends with a full stop which is not entirely accurate. A quick look at texts in the environment (i.e. real texts) shows that many sentences are not completed with a full stop, particularly if they are signs or newspaper headlines.

## Exploring language through play

Early years educators can develop children's natural inclination for talking in role by planning role play areas where the educators model language conventions. Before children can write grammatically correct English, with the appropriate punctuation, they need a lot of experience of talking in their play, using spoken language in many different scenarios.

Opportunities for exploring formal talk and how language works arise naturally for young children through play. In the example in Figure 16.1, a group of four five-year-old children were playing in the shop and book areas. Harry and Rajesh are boys and Jamila and Anna are girls.

## Four and five year olds

### Café role play[5]

The Foundation Stage team had decided to provide a café role play where children would take on the different roles of waiter, customer and chef. The educators wanted the children to learn to speak according to each particular role. The team knew that they needed to prepare the children before setting up the role play, so a visit to a local café was organised where all the children observed what was happening and were encouraged to listen carefully to the waiter when she took their order.

### Café role play – session one

The children are sitting in a large circle to discuss what they saw and heard at the café and then decide what they need for their café. Large pieces of paper are placed in the middle of the circle and every child has some post-it notes and a black marker pen.

To start the session the educator asks the children to talk in talk partners about their visit. She then asks them if they can remember what the waiter asked them. The educator invites the children to write down what they need for the café so that

---

3   Hall N (1998) *Punctuation in the Primary School*. Reading and Language Information Centre, University of Reading, Reading, UK.

4   *Op cit*.

5   Parker.C. (2008) *Stepping into someone else's shoes: DVD and Guidance Notes*. Peterborough Local Authority, UK.

Figure 16.1: Children engaged in shop play, learning the language conventions for different roles

| Description | Commentary |
|---|---|
| *Harry introduces himself.* | |
| **Harry:** Would you like a cup of tea? I've stirred it very well but if you need to stir it some more ... Here you are. | Harry imitates adult talk; he knows the conventions of looking after a visitor. In this scenario the visitor is the educator. |
| **Rajesh:** This says /c/ /l/ /o/. | Rajesh attempts to read the "closed" sign using his phonic knowledge. Educators need to listen out for these opportunities because they provide evidence of consolidated learning. |
| **Jamila:** It says "closed". | |
| *The children decide to turn it over.* | |
| **Jamila:** Here's your things. | |
| **Rajesh:** Can I now please be the shopkeeper? | Rajesh uses the convention of polite speech to negotiate his turn as the shopkeeper. |
| **Jamila:** I've only just got here. | |
| **Rajesh:** Please, please, I've never ever been the shopkeeper. | Rajesh uses persuasive speech to state his case. |
| **Anna:** I haven't either. | |
| **Jamila:** Eeny meeny miney mo. | Jamila takes the lead and decides to resolve the dispute. |
| **Anna:** But I'm doing this. | |
| *Rajesh takes over from Jamila as shopkeeper.* | |
| **Rajesh:** That's okay, you don't need to spend your money at the Tesco. | Rajesh's talk appears to relate to what he has heard adults say. |
| *Rajesh puts Anna's shopping through the scanner.* | |
| **Anna:** You've already done that one ... But I will have some bread. | The dialogue between Rajesh and Anna flows and reflects adult talk. |
| *Rajesh picks up the telephone and dials a number saying the numbers out loud.* | |
| **Rajesh:** Hello, this is Tom. | |
| *Rajesh is interrupted by Jamila.* | |
| **Rajesh:** You have to go round there ... Ohhh I have a ringer ... hello Tom, Rajesh speaking ... hello ... yes ... yes ... yes. | Rajesh appears to represent the supermarket. |
| *As Rajesh speaks on the phone he swipes the goods through the scanner.* | Here, Rajesh is speaking on behalf of the shop. He switches from one to the other. Rajesh is able to replicate adults' telephone talk, allowing for the 'person' on the other end of the line to respond. This is a convention children pick up very quickly. |
| **Rajesh:** Yes ... yes ... yes. Thank you for shopping at Tesco ... yes ... yes ... yes ... see you! | |

# GRAMMAR AND PUNCTUATION

a list can be made. The children like having post-its and marker pens because this reflects what adults have: they write their words down enthusiastically. One by one the children place their post-its on the long piece of paper. If their idea has already been suggested they just place it alongside. The educator has some of the props to hand so that she creates a feeling of anticipation.

## Café role play – session two

A focus group of children is chosen to set up the café with the educator. As they do this she reminds them of what they did yesterday and uses the list of suggestions they made as a prompt and point of reference. When they have finished, a colleague joins the class and together the two adults perform a role play for all the children. The children enjoy this and are excited about having time in the café themselves.

## Café role play – session three

A group of children is invited to play in the café role play area. Because of all the preparation – the visit, setting up the area and observing the educators modeling the language – the children are soon busy. Here are some examples of the language they use:

> Aims for using café language
> with four to five year olds
>
> Teaching aims
>
> • To engage in role play using different language structures appropriately, according to the role.
>
> • To understand that you use different words and sentences depending on the social context.
>
> Assessment evidence in children's language
>
> • Taking on the role of a waiter: "I'm the waiter and I have to take orders".
>
> • "What you want?"
>
> • Taking on the role of customer: "I want sausages and chips, please".

"Cup cakes, would you like a lemon?"
"Um."

"Do you want some cheese?"
"I want cheese."

"We need some plates."
"I don't know if we've got enough food."

"I can put in a cake."
"Leave them on the table until you've finished eating."

When children have had a range of learning experiences where they can become increasingly familiar with different language conventions in oral contexts, they are then ready to move onto developing their writing, taking into account the effective use of grammar and punctuation.

The following illustrations show how children have worked to improve their writing before they write their finished piece, self-correcting during the writing process and revisiting grammar and punctuation.

# Six year olds

## We all like to be beside the seaside!

A Year 2 class visited the seaside. Before writing their accounts of the visit and information about the beach, the children were provided with opportunities to draw the sequence of events and to plan their forthcoming information writing.

The children wrote an account of their visit. Faiza self-corrected her work, as shown in Figure 16.2. She self-corrected words to improve the quality of her writing. For example, she changed "Then we" to "At last". She also checked for capital letters and full stops.

Faiza followed her plan to write an information sheet about *The Seaside* (see Figures 16.3 and 16.4 respectively). In the latter, she again self-corrected her grammar and punctuation as part of the writing process. For example, she corrected "you can by ice creams in ice cream trucks" to "... from

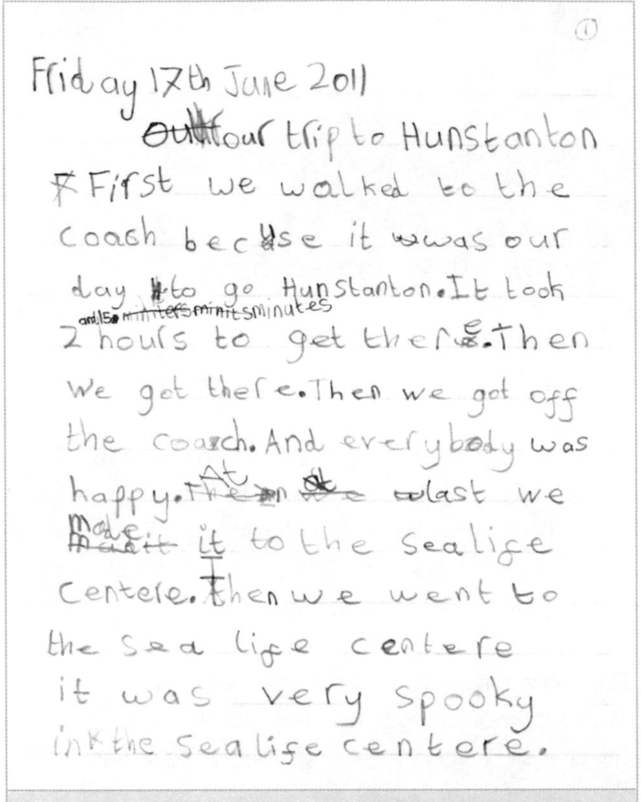

Figure 16.2: Faiza's account, *Our Trip to Hunstanton*

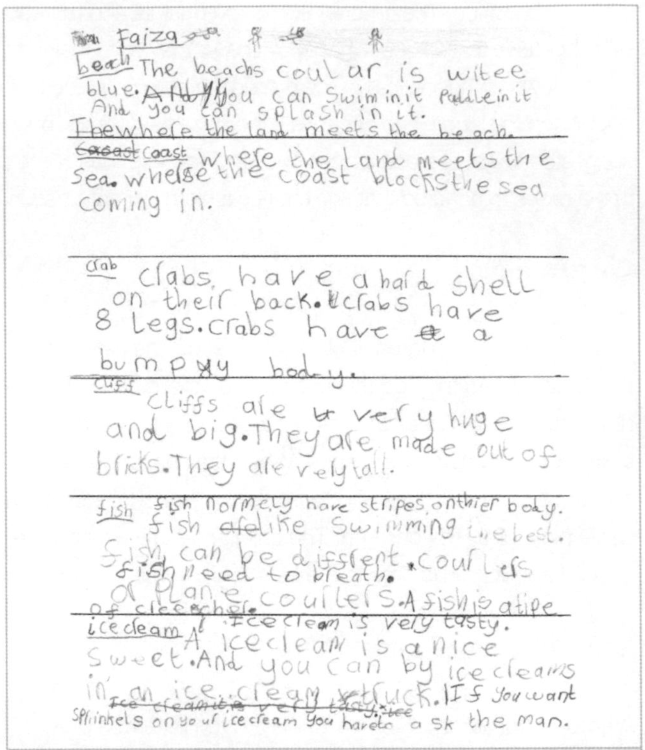

Figure 16.3: Faiza's information writing plan for *The Seaside*

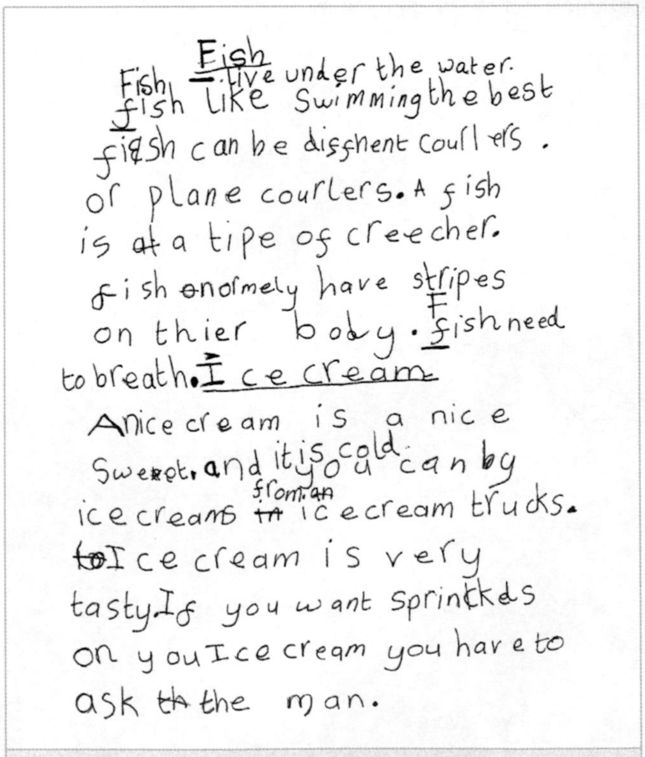

ice cream trucks". She also corrected capital letters at the beginning of sentences, for example changing "fish" to "Fish".

## People who work in school

A class of six year olds thought about the different people who worked in their school. They interviewed staff members, made their own ID badges, and planned improvements for different areas of the school. The ideas were illustrated on 'idea boards', and the children also designed vehicles for travelling to school.

The children all had the opportunity to create their own books about people who work in school. The first versions were created on the computer, including an illustration of each adult.

Neann (see Figure 16.5) drew Miss Stanley (a teacher), Miss Marvin (an office secretary) and Miss Paul (an IT teacher). The children then revisited their books to edit punctuation such as the capital letters and full stops (see Figure 16.6 for Neann's revised version).

Figure 16.4: Faiza's information sheet for *The Seaside*

# GRAMMAR AND PUNCTUATION

people who  work in school

neann

mis stanley is a teach

miss marvin is a offis tech

mis  paul is  a  ist teach

Figure 16.5: Neann's book,
*People Who Work in School*

People who  work in school .

Neann

Mis stanley is a teach.

Miss Marvin is a offis tech.

Mis Paul is  a  ist teach.

Figure 16.6: Neann's book with
capitals and full stops added

Thursday 28th April 2011
Our visit to the Park
First we Left Shool then we work. Next (walked)
we saw the cherch. Then we work in The
Path. second we cross The Road
Afer That I saw Trafick Tight.
I saw Jawllys ShoP I like the
Jawllys ShoP. Then I saw cars in
the road. Later on I saw a beaful
Gard it has beaful flowers and
Grass. on the Way I saw a ShoP
clows it has SPacling closs was
beaful. I saw Lots of Food
I saws APPerl banan and Pese carrot.

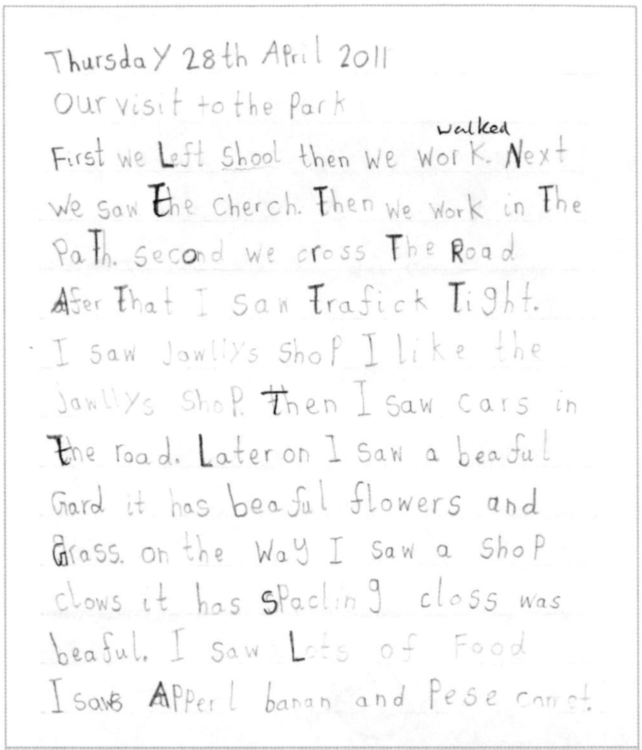

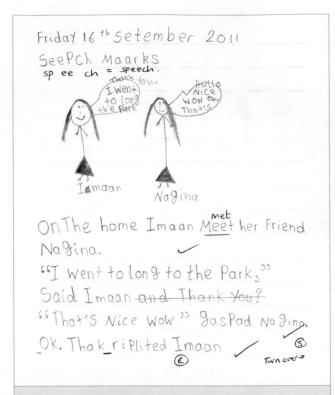

**Figure 16.7: Nagina's *Visit to the Park* with her own edits**

**Figure 16.8: Children's conversations on the way home**

## Our visit to the park

The most effective way of supporting children to improve their grammar and punctuation is to give them time to edit their own work. In Figure 16.7 Nagina revisits her account of a visit to the park. In some respects she over-edits and puts in capital letters where they are not required. This is part of the learning process and with more experience and written and oral responses from the educator she will learn the standard conventions, in relation to the meaning of her written text.

## On the way home ...

To further develop the children's confidence in writing speech and in using speech marks the educator used the story, *On the Way Home* by Jill Murphy[6]. The children had heard the story several times. In talk partners they thought about the conversations that they have on the way home. They drew illustrations showing themselves and their friend walking home after school and used speech bubbles for their talk (see Figure 16.8). The children were then asked to write a short account of their meeting.

6 Murphy J (1982) *On the Way Home*. Macmillan's Children's Books, London, UK.

CHAPTER 17

# Spelling

Within the context of a core story, Zakiyah uses prompts provided in the classroom to improve her spelling

Spelling, particularly spelling in the English language, is dominated by history and convention. In many cases non-standard English spelling communicates meaning without ambiguity. However, there are strong societal pressures for correct or standard spelling, and it is true that until children have mastered standard spelling they cannot be said to be fully competent writers. It is also the case that in order to write well in general, children need to be able to use standard spellings with fluency[1].

Spelling is an area of knowledge about writing that is either caught or taught. Some children seem to catch spelling with relatively little support, while others require a great deal of support. This means that educators need to differentiate their teaching strategies with individuals and groups in order to match teaching with children's assessed needs. An emphasis on invented spelling or the 'have a go' approach is one useful strategy for learners at the early stages of development. However, this emphasis should not be to the exclusion of other more direct teaching approaches because different children will respond better to different approaches, dependent on their stages of development[2].

Teaching spelling requires a clear focus on words and the letter patterns that words are built from. In the early stages

1   Graham S, Morphy P, Harris K, Fink-Chorzempa B, Saddler S M, Mason L (2008) Teaching spelling in the primary grades: A national survey of instructional practices and adaptations. *American Educational Research Journal*, 45(3), 796-825.

2   Martello J (2004) Precompetence and trying to learn: Beginning writers talk about spelling. *Journal of Early Childhood Literacy*, 4, 271-289.

phonological knowledge is important. But quite soon children need to learn that English spelling has complex patterns of sound symbol correspondences. The ability to use standard spelling requires understanding of elements such as word stems, word functions, and grammatical meanings supported by visual memory.

Classic word games such as Scrabble or Hangman can be a motivating way to naturally explore standard spellings. Games designed by educators to support spelling can also be productive. Words on cards and mini whiteboards can be discussed. One of the key elements of the educator's approach to spelling should be to encourage children to see patterns in related groups of words[3].

One area of debate has been the merits of spelling tests. Unfortunately the issues of self-esteem that can be caused by insensitive use of tests have obscured some clear benefits of working with lists of words. Tests should of course only be used when the educator has an assessment or diagnostic purpose in mind. However, a portfolio of a child's writing over time should be able to provide equally good information.

There is value, however, in children working on spelling lists that emphasise particular patterns of words collaboratively to identify standard and non-standard spellings. Words on cards can be used for games such as Pelmanism (sometimes called Pairs or Memory). Words can be searched for in printed materials. Words can also be spelled out loud to reinforce visual memory.

Developmentally, learning to spell using conventional spellings takes considerable time. Some children acquire some basic spelling knowledge as young as four, but for most children their awareness of conventional spellings grows alongside their development of knowledge about letters and sounds from age five onwards. Once children are engaging in phonics sessions in the setting, they become increasingly aware of spelling conventions. It is a key role of educators to draw children's attention to the patterns of spelling and the possibilities and limitations of spelling 'rules'.

## Developing spelling in the continuous provision areas

Children's awareness of spelling conventions can be developed in the different areas of continuous provision by:

- Providing signs for outdoor play that have a purpose such as Keep Out! Builders at work. Children need materials to produce their own signs.

- Lists of resources written in alphabetical order, for example: In the small world area we can play with:

  - Dinosaurs
  - Doll's house figures
  - Doll's house furniture
  - Farm animals
  - Vehicles
  - Wild animals.

## Developing spelling in the writing area

Children's awareness of spelling conventions can be developed in the writing area by providing:

- Alphabets presented in different formats, including zigzag books, small charts and alphabet strips.

- Blank alphabet books for children to create their own dictionaries.

- Copies of the class list for children to use to copy each others' names, including staff names.

- Word lists as prompts for children when writing, including words that have been a focus in phonics and spelling sessions.

- Word banks presented in file boxes. Children can make their own word bank.

---

3    Schlagal B (2007) Best practices in spelling and handwriting. In S Graham, C MacArthur, J Fitzgerald (eds) *Best Practices in Writing Instruction*. Guildford Press, New York, USA.

# SPELLING

- Displays of tongue twisters to motivate children to write their own.

- Materials for children to make their own spelling fans, using card and split pins. They write a list of words that follow the same pattern, then take several fan-shaped pieces of card to write the words neatly and to illustrate. The cards are then joined together with a split pin. The children use the spelling fans to play spelling games with their friends.

- Pre-prepared spelling lists showing different spelling patterns for the children to illustrate and add to.

Working alongside children in the writing area, introduce children to look/cover/say/write/check. The child looks at the word they want to learn to spell, they cover it up with a piece of paper, they say the word, they write the word and check if they have spelt it correctly. In this way the child is able to practise words they are struggling with in a way that is non-threatening and also means they learn to spell the word.

## Developing spelling in the reading area

Children's awareness of spelling conventions can be developed in the reading area by providing:

- A range of alphabet books, such as *Superhero ABC*[4] and *Bob's ABC*[5]

- Different levels of dictionaries, from first dictionaries to junior dictionaries, such as the *Collins First School Dictionary*[6], the *Oxford First Dictionary*[7], *Oxford Junior Dictionary*[8]

- Poetry cards with colour coded letters to highlight patterns in spelling

- Rhyming stories, such as *The Giant Jam Sandwich*[9].

## Four year olds

### Spelling sessions

In Chapter 12 we described a series of phonics sessions using a puppet character. Spelling can be taught in a similar way and in the early stages is closely related to teaching phonics. In this series of spelling sessions a puppet called Ali the Alligator, the top spelling investigator, is used!

### Spelling – session one

The children are introduced to Ali the Alligator, who is going to help them improve their spelling. The educator shows the children a page in the core book of the week and asks the children to read a sentence that the educator has selected. One of the children is then invited to point to the word 'owl' in the sentence.

Having linked the beginning of the session to a whole text, the focus of the first session is on 'ow' words such as 'brown', 'crown' and 'down'. The children are asked to add to the list. Some children will suggest words that are spelled with the letters 'ou', such as 'out'. These should be added to the list because this reflects the way that English spelling works: the same sound can often be written with different spellings. At other times it is important to make the focus exclusively on the letter pattern (in this case it would mean sticking only to words spelled with the letters 'ow'). In talk partners children write their own lists of 'ow' words using handheld whiteboards. The children are given the challenge to make up a sentence using as many 'ow' words as possible. They share their ideas which are scribed ready to refer to the next day.

4   McLeod B (2006) *Superhero ABC*. HarperCollins Children's Books, New York, USA.

5   Bartram S (2005) *Bob's ABC*. Templar Publishing, Dorking, UK.

6   Graham J, Lister M *Collins First School Dictionary*. HarperCollins Publishers, London, UK.

7   Delahunty A (2011) *Oxford First Dictionary*. Oxford University Press, Oxford, UK.

8   Dignen S (2007) *Oxford Junior Dictionary*. Oxford University Press, Oxford, UK.

9   Vernon Lord J (1972) *The Giant Jam Sandwich*. Red Fox: Random House Children's Books, London, UK.

**A treasure hunt for words that have 'th'.
One child finds 'thick'**

## Spelling – session two

Ali the Alligator returns to read out the children's 'ow' sentences. In their talk partners the children improve on their sentences. The children are encouraged to use each others' ideas and to see who can make the longest sentence. Ali challenges the children by asking them to write the longest sentence on their individual whiteboards. How many times have they spelt the 'ow' words conventionally? Some children are directed to the writing area to look/cover/say/write/check 'ow' words. Another group goes to find 'ow' words in books in the book area.

## Spelling – session three

Ali the Alligator tells the children that they are going to focus on words spelled with the letters 'ow' that make the sound /oh/. Ali shows some examples from texts in the book area, for example stories and poems with words such as 'glow', 'slow', 'crow', 'hollow' and 'follow'. Ali the Alligator sets the children a challenge. There are 'ow' word cards hidden inside and outside. The children have to find as many of the words as they can, and to collect the words and save them for the next session.

## Spelling – session four

The children present the 'ow' word cards they have found to Ali the Alligator. Together they read all the words and pass them round to have a closer look. Next, a quick game is played. Using a timer (a sand timer or some other type including online digital versions), the children work with partners to see how many 'ow' words they can spell conventionally in three minutes. They check their answers and then the children are given the challenge again but in two minutes. The amount of time is varied according to the level of the children's spelling and how quickly the educator wants the children to write.

## Spelling – session five

The children's success in spelling 'ow' words is celebrated. Ali the Alligator performs a story using as many 'ow' words as possible. The children have to tally every time they hear an 'ow' word and then at the end write down as many 'ow' words as possible. Here's an example of a story that could be used.

One night a brown owl was flying across the dark sky over the deep snow. There was a glow in the distance. The brown owl flew slowly towards the mysterious glow. At the same time, like an arrow, a black crow darted across the sky. The black crow was flying towards the glow in the sky too. A swallow sat in the highest branch of an old oak tree. The swallow flew towards the glow too. The three birds met at the source of the glow. It was a golden crown. "Who does that belong to?" asked the frowning brown owl.

"Let's take it to the tall tower. I think we will find the owner of the crown in the tall tower."

Together the three birds carried the golden crown up, up into the dark sky and far into the night until they came to the tall tower. There, dressed in a silver flowery gown, was a princess. She was weeping. The princess looked up and saw the party of birds arriving.

"It's my crown!" she called.

The three birds landed on the tall tower. They bowed and presented the golden crown to the princess.

# SPELLING

"Oh thank you, thank you!" the princess cried.

The children are given time to share their tallies and words with their talk partner. A few pairs are chosen to feed back to the whole class. The children are then given the text so that they can highlight the 'ow' words. This is differentiated by giving different children either a sentence, a few sentences or the whole text to work on.

## Games and strategies to develop spelling

- Create word (or 'treasure') hunts outside, where children have to find words with the same spelling pattern such as 'ing'. When they find one, they have to mime the relevant action – for example digging or mixing.

- Make collections of objects that share the same spelling pattern for the children to label and write about. Play Kim's Game: the memory game where you cover objects with a cloth, remove one object, then and see if anyone can say what is missing.

- Play I Spy with a focus on a specific word pattern such as words that rhyme with 'spring': for example I spy a picture of a king, I spy a bird's wing, I spy the prince's bling, I spy some string.

- Provide ready-made memory games, and blank cards for children to make up their own. Children will often create more challenging games, trying to catch each other out.

- Use Lotto games to reinforce specific word patterns. Provide opportunities for the children to create their own Lotto games using blank boards and cards.

- Look at a text and use highlighters to show different spelling patterns and word groups.

- Look at a text and use highlighters to show irregular words that break spelling 'rules'.

- Use dictionaries to find words with the same spelling pattern. Find out what the words mean.

- Look for words within words. Prompts can be provided in writing areas.

- Clap the syllables of words such as animal names: bear, ti-ger, e-le-phant, al-li-ga-tor. Support with books in the book area such as *Tanka Tanka Skunk!*[10].

## Six year olds

### Case study: A child's journey to better spelling

Haseeb is six years old. Figures 17.1 to 17.3 demonstrate how he became a more confident writer and in the process developed his spelling over time.

In the first sample of his writing (Figure 17.1), Haseeb is able to spell the words "my", "and" and "Haseeb" correctly. He reverses a /b/ and writes "dig" for big. He writes "bruder" for brother and "cord" for called.

In the second sample (Figure 17.2), Haseeb can spell consonant vowel consonant words, such as "mum", "van" and "let". He can spell more complex words, for example "brother", "games" and "everything". He attempts his own spelling, such as "ics crearm" for ice cream and "cersunt" for cousin.

In the third sample (Figure 17.3), Haseeb is beginning to self-correct. He has drawn wavy lines under "hegogs" for hedgehogs and "bord" for bored, knowing that these are incorrect.

---

10 Webb S (2003) *Tanka, Tanka, Skunk!* Red Fox: Random House Children's Books, London, UK.

L/Obj -To be able to write independently about "My Family"

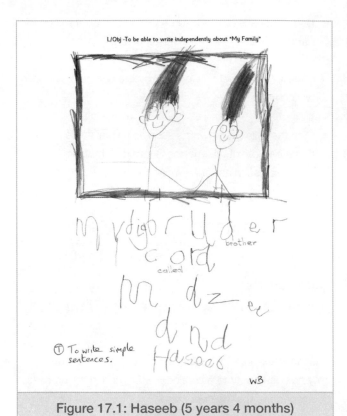

My digor Uder brother

cord called

M dz ee

d nd

Hdseeb

① To write simple sentences.

WB

**Figure 17.1: Haseeb (5 years 4 months) writes about his family**

Haseeb

My FAMLY    24.05.2010

alser  dad  Foxy  mi  safee

My mum  My Brother is kiny. My dad is a icecrearm van. My mum likse tooco My brouther likse to play my citer do jobs. mi cer the brou play loys to play t u. my dad rive me everything. my cusun let me play his gum es my dad is so old.

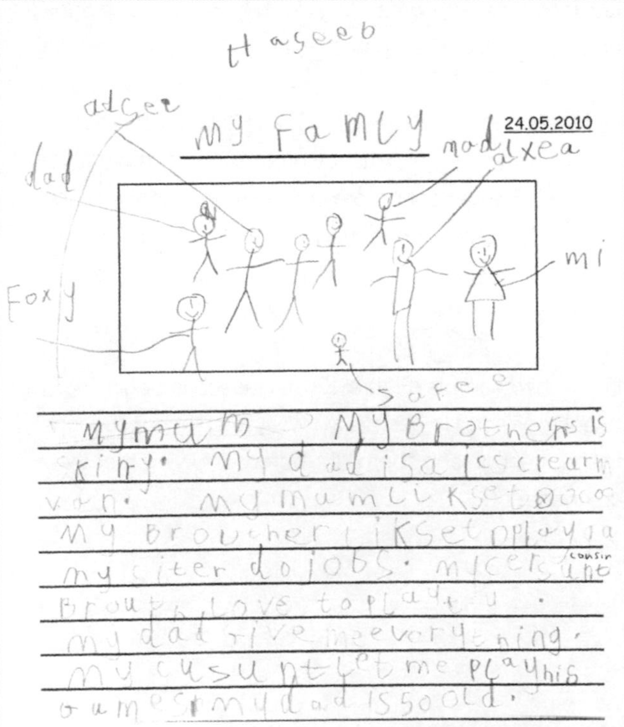

**Figure 17.2: Haseeb (6 years 2 months) writes about his family**

night-time

Haseeb          07 04 2011

we go to sleep at night Some time i play whith my games. FFox come out at night because they look for their prery My mum cooks at night. Shops some times out at night because if you need something Owls come out at night heggs come out at night cat come out at night Some times i play whith my sisters because when you get bord bats come out at night Some times i work at night because its good i do that everyday my dad drives a taxi at night because some people if they get stuk Iysometimes go at night

Some time i see owls i don't sleep at night I think bagers come at night? Some times i see bom fires

fireworks

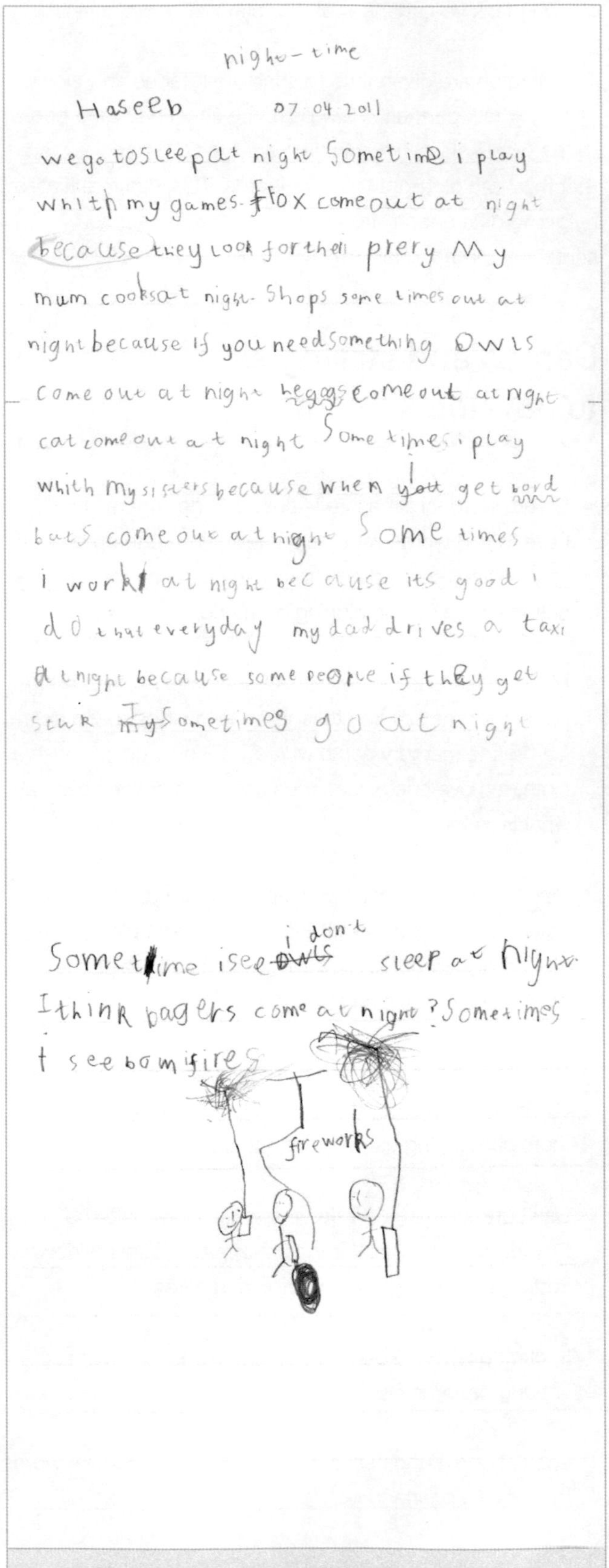

**Figure 17.3: Haseeb (7 years 1 month) writes about night time**

CHAPTER 18

# Handwriting

Writing on a large scale helps children to understand directionality

There is increasing evidence of the importance of handwriting to writing processes generally. Fluent handwriting benefits the composition of writing[1]. Handwriting is a skill that needs to be taught on a regular basis, which will mean short daily sessions focussing specifically on handwriting[2]. Learning to form the individual letters of the alphabet and produce legible handwriting at a reasonable speed involves a complex perceptuo-motor skill. The goal of handwriting teaching is a legible, fluent and comfortable style. Legibility requires different standards, according to the purpose of the writing[3]. For example, personal note taking only needs to be readable by the person who makes the notes.

Posture and working space are important elements of handwriting. For right-handed pupils, the paper is tilted to about 45 degrees anti-clockwise. It is important that the writing implement is not gripped too hard as this can lead to muscle tension in the shoulder and pain in the wrist and hand. It is important to be aware of all the left-handed children in the class from the beginning of the year. As far as handwriting is concerned, left-handed children have particular needs. Their writing moves inwardly, i.e. in towards their bodies, thus tending to make it difficult for them to read what they have just written. Left-handers should be encouraged to turn their paper clockwise (to

1   Medwell J, Wray D (2010) Handwriting and writing. In D Wyse, R Andrews, J Hoffman (eds) *The Routledge International Handbook of English, Language and Literacy Teaching*. Routledge, London, UK.

2   Schlagel B (2007) Best practices in spelling and handwriting. In S Graham, C MacArthur, J Fitzgerald (eds) *Writing Instruction*. Guildford Press, New York, USA.

3   Sassoon R (2003) *Handwriting: The way to teach it*. Second Edition. Paul Chapman Publishing, London, UK.

about 45 degrees), not to hold their pen or pencil too near to the actual point and to sit on a chair that is high enough to allow them good visibility. Left-handers can be helped by ensuring that they sit to the left of a right-hander so that their elbows are not competing for space.

Direction, movement and height are all crucial: left to right and top to bottom; the fact that letters have prescribed flowing movements with specific starting and exit points; the necessity to ensure that letters have particular height differences. In addition, the variance between upper and lower case must be recognised and correct spacing consistently applied. Particular care has to be taken when teaching certain letters that are mirror images of each other, such as b-d, m-w, n-u and p-q, to avoid confusion for young learners. Speed – but not too much speed – is important as this can lead to fluency and greater efficiency[4].

Opportunities to write on a large scale help younger children to understand directionality. Examples include using decorator paintbrushes with water, large flowing movements in the sand, fingerpaints, gloop, and writing in the air. All these activities help children to feel unrestricted and achieve a feeling of success. At the same time, educators demonstrate handwriting as role models whenever they write in the setting. In the early years setting educators record their observations daily. Children notice this and like to ask "What are you doing?" This provides an opportunity to explain what they are doing with writing while it is in process. As children become familiar with the educator's purposes for writing observations they may ask the educator to record specific events and aspects of their learning. Some children will imitate observation writing. All these moments provide an opportunity to talk about and reinforce handwriting and writing more generally.

Teaching children each letter methodically helps them to see the connections in letter formation between different groups of letters. Using individual whiteboards helps children to make their mark without hesitating too much, because it can be simply rubbed out and practised again. Children often enjoy engaging in writing during a circle time, where all the educators can provide support and

encouragement. Orally describing the action and direction of the marks helps children to form letters conventionally. For example, "Letter 'I': start at the top, then straight down". To help children understand that there are times when the quality of handwriting is particularly important, educators can provide opportunities for them to contribute to the environmental print in the classroom. For example, a child might need to write a "Please Keep Off" notice for a model made in the construction area. When children know that writing a polite notice is an option, they will come up with many suggestions for the wording themselves. When a daily question is prepared for the children, the educator can progress from expecting children to write their names under 'yes' and 'no' answers to answers that require more words and more complex answers. On a daily basis children can sign up to take turns in activities that are especially popular and cannot always be available to everyone, such as having a turn on the interactive whiteboard or on a favourite tricycle. In Chapter 6 Rehan wrote his name for a turn on the interactive whiteboard. In the image at the start of Chapter 9, all the children in a Year 1 class signed their class charter.

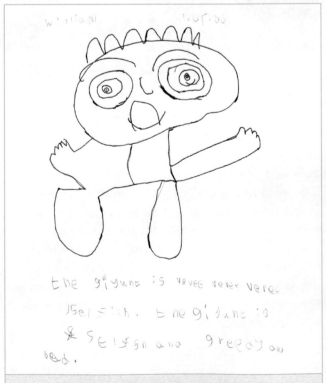

**Figure 18.1: A giant illustration with accompanying words**

---

4   *Op cit.*

# HANDWRITING

Opportunities to write cards for friends and family provide another real situation where children will focus on the quality of their writing. This activity needs to be on-going in an early years setting. Children are keen to write notes to the educator and are intrinsically motivated to do this. The realisation that some written messages communicate more effectively than others is a spur to the children's curiosity, and something that naturally leads to the need for conventional writing. The need for communication over distances, the need for good record-keeping and hence the need for shared conventions, were the main reasons that written language developed in the way that it did historically. Communicating meaning in a way that is clearly understood by the recipient (no matter how strange it may look to others – for example, the use of things like emoticons in teenagers' text messages) is still the driving force of all language.

Children are also keen to contribute to classroom displays. One class focussed on the story of *Jack and the Beanstalk*. Children drew illustrations of the giant and then labelled their pictures to describe them for the display. (see Figure 18.1).

As children become more capable in writing, formal letter writing can be introduced.

Providing real purposes makes the task more enjoyable and enhances the children's learning. Examples include writing a letter to say thank you to a visitor to the setting; to their families about an up-and-coming event; to the school council about something they want for the school; or perhaps to ask for a resource from a local supermarket or business. Educators will often have a soft toy, perhaps a teddy bear, that the children take home, take photographs of and then write a diary entry for. Space Raccoon features in one setting where the children's contributions are collated in a large class book.

In addition to the other writing that older children carry out, including for real purposes, they will sometimes edit their writing to present a display or to make a class book. All children need to learn to control the presentational aspects of both handwriting and computer-generated texts. The examples in Figures 18.2 and 18.3 are from a class project about belonging. The seven-year-old children wrote up poems about the autumn leaves they had collected in the school grounds.

Figure 18.2: Zainab's poem about an autumn leaf

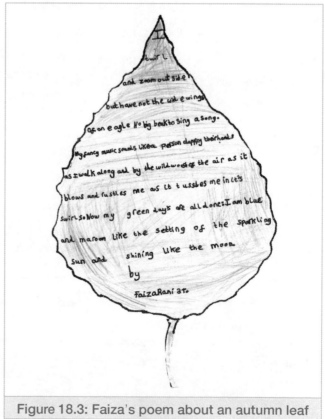

Figure 18.3: Faiza's poem about an autumn leaf